By Regina Hall

Copyright

Copyright @ 2024, Regina Hall

All rights reserved. No part of this book may be reproduced, stored, or transmitted by any means—whether auditory, graphic, mechanical, or electronic—without written permission of both publisher and author, except in the case of brief excerpts used in critical articles and reviews. Unauthorized reproduction of any part of this work is illegal and punishable by law.

Because of the dynamic nature of the Internet, any web addresses or links contained in this book may have changed since publication and may no longer be valid.

Hard Cover ISBN-13: 979-8-9912211-0-8

eBook ISBN: 979-8-9912211-1-5

Published in 2024 by:

Echoes in Healing

Virginia Beach, Virginia

Disclaimer

This book is based on true events and real people. The events described are as accurate as possible to the best of the author's memory. However, in some instances, names, locations, and identifying details have been changed to protect the privacy of individuals. Any resemblance to actual persons, living or dead, or actual events not depicted in the book is purely coincidental.

The views and opinions expressed in this book are those of the author and do not necessarily reflect the official policy or position of any agency, organization, or individual mentioned. The author has made every effort to ensure the accuracy and completeness of the information contained within the book; however, the author assumes no responsibility for errors, omissions, or contrary interpretation of the subject matter herein.

Readers are advised to use their own discretion when interpreting the events and experiences shared in this book. The author and publisher shall not be held liable for any damages resulting from the use or interpretation of the material presented in this book.

Table of Contents

FOREWORD IX

PREFACE XI

DEDICATIONS XIII

INTRODUCTION 1

CHAPTER 1: BEGINNINGS 3

CHAPTER 2: MOVING TO LINDEN BOULEVARD 7

CHAPTER 3: A SANCTUARY IN THE SHADOWS 17

CHAPTER 4: UNVEILING TRUTHS: A JOURNEY FROM SHADOWS TO LIGHT 21

CHAPTER 5: BETRAYAL AND BRAVERY: NAVIGATING LOVE AND LOSS IN 1960S BROOKLYN 27

CHAPTER 6: PILLARS OF STRENGTH: LOVE AND LOSS IN THE SHADOW OF UNCERTAINTY 33

CHAPTER 7: A FATHER'S LOVE: EMBRACING BONDS BEYOND BLOOD 39

CHAPTER 8: ECHOES OF LOVE AND RESILIENCE: A BROOKLYN BEGINNING 45

CHAPTER 9: ENDURING LOVE AND RESILIENCE: NAVIGATING NEW BEGINNINGS 51

CHAPTER 10: BOUND BY LOVE: FAMILY, CHALLENGES, AND UNBREAKABLE BONDS 63

CHAPTER 11: TRANSITIONS AND TRIALS: NAVIGATING NEW BEGINNINGS 75

CHAPTER 12: FORGED IN FAITH: TRIUMPHS AND TRIALS OF FAMILY BONDS 85

CHAPTER 13: RESILIENCE AND REDEMPTION: A JOURNEY OF HOPE AND HEALING 101

CHAPTER 14: THROUGH THE STORM: EMBRACING MOTHERHOOD AND FINDING STRENGTH 117

CHAPTER 15: RUSHED DECISIONS, HARD LESSONS 133

CHAPTER 16: SEEKING REFUGE AND FINDING STRENGTH 143

CONCLUSION AND NEXT STEPS 157

FOLLOW ECHOES IN HEALING	159
REFERENCES FOR THERAPISTS	161
ABOUT THE AUTHOR	163

Foreword

You are about to embark on a journey through the life of Regina (Mitchell) Hall. This autobiography is a testament to the resilience, drive, strong faith, and determination of the author.

Regina is a daughter, mother, grandmother, sister, and friend to many. She has lived a life that has taken her all over the world. She is an entrepreneur and a life coach. She enjoys traveling and spending time with her family and friends, as well as alone time to nurture herself.

As you turn each page you will be taken on a journey of a life that has experienced heartache and pain, triumphs and tribulations, forgiveness and strength, and her ability to withstand it all. She has experienced some of the darkest times and through it all was able to pick herself up and become the strong, loving, inspiring woman that she is today.

You may see yourself in some of these situations or know someone who has endured the same. The author shares her story not to hurt anyone involved but to encourage those who have endured the same heartache, struggles, and life circumstances in hopes that you will be able to reflect on your own life, understand her life a little better, and learn how to love and forgive in the end.

Her story serves as a reminder that no matter what cards you are dealt in life you can create your own narrative and write the rest of your life story the way you want it to be. Her hope is that by telling her story it will inspire others to embrace their own journeys, celebrate their own victories, and heal from their past.

I am looking forward to reading her story even though I have known her for almost 50 years. I know that I will also learn something as I turn these pages and travel on her journey.

This book is the first in a series that she intends to publish so when you get to the end of the book know that it is not the end of her journey and there is more to come.

Thank you, Gina (Regina), for giving me the privilege to write the foreword for your first book.

Love you,

        Jessica

Preface

The journey of writing this book has been one of self-discovery, reflection, and immense learning. "*Pieces of Me*" is not just a collection of stories, but a testament to the resilience and strength that lies within each of us. It spans across decades, highlighting the highs and lows, the struggles and triumphs, and the moments that have shaped me into who I am today.

The idea for this book came to me during a particularly challenging period in my life. I realized that the experiences I had endured and the lessons I had learned could serve as a source of hope for others facing similar trials. My goal in sharing these pieces of my life is to inspire, to heal, and to connect with readers on a deeply personal level.

This book would not have been possible without the constant support of my family and friends. My heartfelt thanks go to my mother, the late Dolores Banks (Lewis), whose strength and wisdom have been my guiding light; my daughters, Sarita, Kayla, and Sierra, whose presence has brought joy even in the darkest times.

To my sister Charmin, if it wasn't for you encouraging me, always using the words, "Do whatever you want to do, sis. I support you," I want you to know that your words of encouragement meant the world to me. Even though you were an author yourself and decided to start a new journey, you passed the torch to me, and for that, I am forever grateful.

Regina Hall

I watched everyone else pursue their paths while I remained silent, not speaking my truth. But thanks to your devoted support and your motto, "Whatever you want to do, sis," I found the courage to embark on my own journey. I love you so much.

I am also grateful to my editor, Betty Norlin, who believed in my vision and helped bring this project to life. Special thanks to my book cover designer, the Creative Visionary OddlyHuman, for helping my vision come to life.

"*Pieces of Me*" is the first of the five-book series, *Echoes in Healing*, each focusing on different aspects of my life and personal growth. From the early years of hardship and survival to the later years of self-discovery and healing, each book represents a chapter in my ongoing journey. I encourage you to take your time with each section, reflect on the stories shared, and perhaps find pieces of your own story within mine.

Writing this preface brings a sense of closure to a long and transformative process. It is my hope that as you read "*Pieces of Me*," you will feel a connection to the themes of resilience, vulnerability, and ultimately, triumph. The next book in this series, "*Naked*," will delve even deeper into the vulnerabilities and self-discoveries that have shaped my path.

Thank you for embarking on this journey with me.

Regina Hall

Dedications

This series is devoted to the cherished memory of my mother, **Dolores Lorraine (Lewis) Banks.** Her wisdom, strength, and enduring spirit continues to guide and inspire me, even though she is no longer physically with us. Her love is teaching, remaining an enduring presence in my life, shaping the person I've become.

This book brings forth the most profound experiences of my life. My mother was a wellspring of wisdom. In times of trouble, she was always the one I would call. She was not only a mother to me, but also to my friends, offering guidance and support when they had no one else to turn to. She was an amazing, strong, and feisty woman.

Mommy, I dedicate this book to you because I miss you so much. In the past, you couldn't always express the words you needed to say due to the battles of hurt and pain that weighed on you. But now, I am your voice. Your children may follow in your shadows, but I am here to tell my story. I aim to break every curse that has transpired, so we no longer have to bear them. Let this be a living testimony.

Even though my siblings, Lorraine and Theodore Junior, affectionately known as Moochie, are no longer here, your legacy stands the test of time. As I continue this story, I dedicate every word to you. I know that by dedicating these words, my intention is not to hurt anyone or to expose anyone, but rather to share the stories that shaped my life and what I have witnessed.

You were a minister, a public figure, and a no-nonsense person who always spoke your truth without hiding behind closed doors. Every word of this first series, "Pieces of Me," is dedicated to you. I love you, Mommy. May your spirit live on forever, and may I continue to live through you. Forever.

The man I have always called father and dad:

My use of the term 'stepfather' in this narrative is purely descriptive and not meant to diminish the pivotal role you have played in my life. Truly, you are my bonus dad. This book includes stories and experiences from my perspective, some of which might be revelations to you. Please know that these reflections are not intended to cause you pain or to question the deep respect and love I have for you.

You have shown remarkable strength and growth, emerging as a powerful man of God, and your journey has been a source of inspiration for me. You will always be the father figure in my life, cherished and respected. As I express everything in this book, it is because I no longer want to live in darkness. But know that this does not define who you are today. You have grown to be who you are because of the challenges you faced in life, from a little boy to a man, and then to a man who took on the responsibility of raising another woman's children.

You did not know how to be a father at the time, and you had to work through many issues from your own life and experiences. The mistakes you made were just that—mistakes. They do not diminish your character or the man you have become. You are still the man I look up to, and that is why you can preach with such conviction.

These are things I had to identify as I watched you, and I no longer want to live with burdens of lies or pretending. I love you with all my heart, and I hope you understand that my intent is not to cause hurt but to share my truth.

To my beautiful daughters, Sarita, Kayla, and Sierra:

You three are the greatest gifts I have ever received, and I adore and love you with all my heart. My children mean the world to me, and I want you to know that no one can ever tell you about your mother better than I can. I have endured much pain while raising you, and I was not a perfect mother, but my love for you was always boundless.

I may not have always been the ideal role model, but I strived to be the best mother I could be. I wanted to be a woman you could look up to, even with my imperfections and mistakes. I want my grandchildren to know who I am, and that only I can tell my story. You were never mistakes, despite what society might say. God doesn't make mistakes, and every experience in my life was meant to shape me and, in turn, shape you.

I tried my best to shield you from the hardships I faced, but I know some of my pain reached you. That pain ran deep, but it also gave me the strength to tell my story in this first book of my series. Know that I cherish you so much, and I want you to understand what I went through and what I witnessed. I share my story not to hold anyone accountable or to cause anger, but to illuminate the life lessons I have learned.

You are my heartbeats, and God blessed me with three beautiful girls who have grown into incredible women. As you read this book, understand that it is not to incite anger or judgment but to share my journey with you. These are life lessons, and I want to prevent any repeats of my struggles in your lives. You are destined to be phenomenal women, and I want you to know that your mother faced many challenges but held on to her faith and love for you.

I didn't turn to anything else because I wanted to be a perfect mom, and while I know I wasn't, I want you to hear my story from beginning to end. Darkness may have lingered, but now it is time for you to see my light. I love you so much, my beloved daughters.

To my cherished grandchildren:

This book may unveil stories about your grandmother that are new to you. I want you to understand that these revelations do not change the boundless love I have for each of you. Generational curses do not define who we are—not me as your grandmother, nor your mothers. Life is a series of learning lessons and unveiling secrets, but I never want to be a mystery to you. My journey, with all its ups and downs, is a testament to growth and the power of love that transcends generations.

As I share my story with you, my precious grandchildren, remember that sometimes people in this world can be jealous and spiteful. Know that your grandmother is not here to judge others harshly, but to enlighten you. People can be very evil, but I want to break all these generational curses that I have witnessed in my life. This includes both men and women.

I am here to tell my story because I believe you will be old enough to understand when you read this first book in the series about my life. As you become young adults, I want you to know everything about your grandmother—no secrets, just love and truth. I cherish you all so deeply.

The word "mother" is powerful, and as your grandmother, whom you call "Ummi," it holds a special place in my heart. I chose this name because I wanted to be different. I became a grandmother at the age of 38, with my first granddaughter, Nevaeh. From that moment, I knew I was meant to be a guiding light for all of you.

I have had the privilege of watching you grow into the wonderful individuals you are meant to be, because that is what God intended. Always remember that Ummi loves you all, deeply and unconditionally.

To my beloved niece and nephews:

You grew up alongside me, and I cared for you throughout my childhood and into adulthood. You hold a special place in my heart, akin to my own children. I want you to know that the role I played in your lives was filled with love and dedication. As a mother figure to you, my love and care for you have been an integral part of my life's journey. My story, as shared in these pages, is also part of your story, and it is told with immense love and respect for each of you.

As I write these words, I want to acknowledge who you all are to me. I have 4 nephews, Jamel and Joshua, and two others, one niece, my beloved niece, whom I raised. I also have two other nephews who did not grow up under my care, but I adore and love each and every one of you deeply.

To Jamel, Joshua, and my beloved niece, I want to express how much I cherish you. Taking on the responsibility of raising you was not a choice I made lightly, but one I embraced out of love. I want you to understand the depth of my commitment and the strength it took to be there for you. Jamel, you hold a special place in my heart. I love our long talks and your understanding. I hope the stories in this book help you heal and grow into the man you are destined to be.

To my beloved niece, even though you chose not to be mentioned in this book, know that I love you in spite of any differences we may have. I faced many challenges and responsibilities that my siblings could not handle, and I did my best to be there for you all.

Joshua, I had to step into a parenting role during the summers you stayed with us, which often extended beyond the summer. I endured many challenges and took on responsibilities to help our family. My mother couldn't do it all alone, so I stepped in to support her.

Pieces of Me

To my other two nephews, whom I do not know as well, I love you just as much and hope that one day we can all come together as a family.

This dedication is to release my pain and to let you know that I love my niece and nephews as if you were my own children. I hope these words bring you understanding and show you the depth of my love and dedication to you all.

To all my loved ones reflected in these pages:

My intention in sharing these stories is not to cause pain or discomfort. These narratives come from a place of honesty, reflection, and love. They are a part of our shared history, filled with moments of resilience, strength, and the transformative power of love and forgiveness. My hope is that by sharing my journey, we can all embrace the lessons learned and move forward with understanding, compassion, and forgiveness.

This is not to cause any divisions. As you read these pages, know that these are truths that need to be told, not left undone. Sometimes, we hide behind various facades, including church, religion, or our backgrounds. But I am here to reveal what really happened in my life, whether you were part of it or not. These are my darkest days as we begin book one of this series. This is not intended to hurt but to journal life, as some of you may be or have been going through similar things.

I am writing my story, and I am glad you are here to read it. Forgiveness—always forgiveness—is hard for certain people, and holding grudges can be easier. But I am not here to hold anything against anyone. Sometimes people can't share a meal at your table or fellowship, but I hope each and every one of you will change and love each other, especially family.

The word 'family' sometimes gets lost, and some people don't know it's true meaning. Some of us are bound by blood, and some are bound by the profound connections we forge. Here is what 'family' means to me:

F – Forgiveness: Always finding it in our hearts to forgive one another.

A – Acceptance: Embracing each other's flaws and differences without judgment.

M – Memories: Cherishing the moments we share and the experiences that bind us.

I – Inspiration: Encouraging and uplifting each other to be the best versions of ourselves.

L – Love: The unconditional and steady bond that holds us together.

Y – Yearning: The desire to always stay connected, no matter the distance or time.

I love each and every one of you.

Introduction

I am Regina (Mitchell) Hall, a native New Yorker, born in Long Island College Hospital on May 20th, 1968, in Brooklyn, New York. My mother, Dolores Lorraine Mitchell (Lewis), was 27 years old. She grew up in the Red Hook projects in a household of seven, with her parents married and having one daughter (my mom) and four sons. As a Bay Ridge High School graduate, my mother's spirit was unyielding. She rebelled against the constraints of her strict upbringing, often finding comfort away from home, seeking refuge with the Harrington's. The Harrington's were not just acquaintances; they were practically family to my mother. As a teenager, she found comfort and belonging within their tight-knit circle. The Harrington's, composed of sisters and brothers, welcomed her with open arms, giving her a sense of home away from home. Among the Harrington's, my mother's high school sweetheart was one of the brothers. Their bond ran deep, woven with the threads of youthful romance and shared experiences. The Harrington's embraced my mother as one of their own, blurring the lines between friendship and kinship. They became her adopted family in many ways, offering support, love, and companionship during her formative years.

Chapter 1: Beginnings

From the Red Hook projects to the brownstone, growing up on Waverly Avenue in Brooklyn, New York, was a vibrant and formative experience. The Red Hook Projects, located in the southwestern part of Brooklyn, were where my early years were spent. My mother, an African American woman of strength and resilience, faced many challenges with grace and determination. She ensured that each of us—my sister Lorraine, who was eight years old, my brother Moochie, who was seven, and myself, the youngest—felt loved and cared for.

When I came home from the hospital, it was to 448 Waverly Avenue, Brooklyn, NYC. Waverly Avenue, which runs through the neighborhoods of Clinton Hill and Bedford-Stuyvesant, became our new home. This area is known for its historic brownstones, tree-lined streets, and vibrant community atmosphere. Eventually, we moved to 24 Sterling Place, another cherished street that added to the fabric of our neighborhood experiences.

The neighborhood was alive with the energy and culture of New York City. Our days were filled with the joyful chaos of block parties, where neighbors gathered to celebrate and dance to the latest music. I remember the excitement of playing in the open fire hydrants, pretending they were swimming pools. The cold water provided a refreshing escape from the summer heat as we ran and laughed, splashing through the streams.

Regina Hall

We lived in classic Brooklyn brownstones, navigating the city streets with the sounds of streetcars and taxis beeping their horns as the soundtrack of our daily life. The air was filled with the melodies of the city, a blend of music, conversations, and the hustle and bustle of urban life.

Double Dutch was a favorite pastime. We would gather on the sidewalks, jumping between the ropes with skill and rhythm, showing off our best moves. Dancing was another way we expressed our joy and creativity, moving to the beats that seemed to resonate through the very streets we called home.

My mother, ever watchful and caring, was our anchor. Despite the difficulties she faced, she made sure our childhood was filled with love, warmth, and a sense of belonging. She navigated the complexities of motherhood with a grace that was nothing short of inspirational.

Pieces of Me

"I AM RESILIENT & CAPABLE OF OVERCOMING ANY CHALLENGE"

PIECES OF ME

Regina Hall

PIECES OF ME

Chapter 2: Moving to Linden Boulevard

After Raymond, a cherished part of our family, passed away, we moved from Waverly Avenue to Linden Boulevard in Brooklyn, NYC. This street became a new chapter in our lives, imbued with the vibrant culture and sense of community that Brooklyn is renowned for. Eventually, we relocated to Lowell, Massachusetts, and then to Chelmsford, Massachusetts. Despite these changes, the memories of our time in Brooklyn—the sense of community, the vibrant culture, and the love that held us together—remained a central part of our lives.

As I journey back to our life on Linden Boulevard in Brooklyn, memories flood my mind like fragments of a forgotten dream. The street was always bustling with life, a tapestry of diverse faces and stories. The sound of children playing, the aroma of different cuisines wafting from open windows, and the lively chatter of neighbors made Linden Boulevard feel like the heartbeat of our community.

In our household, these days were marked by my mother's fascination with horoscopes. She wasn't necessarily a passionate believer in astrology, but she was deeply intrigued by the insights it offered. Often, I would find her immersed in horoscope books, not viewing the stars as guiding forces but rather as symbols that could offer glimpses into the personalities of others or provide intriguing narratives to explore. Her interest in horoscopes left a significant imprint on our household, shaping conversations and sparking curiosity in all of us.

Our time on Linden Boulevard was more than just a period in our lives; it was a formative experience that taught us about the richness of diversity and the importance of community. It was there that we learned to navigate life's challenges together, drawing strength from the bonds we shared and the love that enveloped us. These memories, though distant, remain a cherished part of our collective story, reminding us of the vibrant life we once lived on Linden Boulevard.

As I reminisce about those days, I realize how my mother's exploration of horoscopes added a layer of curiosity and intrigue to our home. Her interest in astrology sparked lively conversations and provided a lens through which to view the intricacies of human nature. In the tapestry of her life on Linden Boulevard, her interest in horoscopes was a colorful thread that wove its way through her daily experiences, enriching her understanding of the world and the people within it. I recall how she decided to have a painting created that captured her devotion to astrology. The painting, adorned with the Taurus bull, intricately portrayed the birth signs of her children. Each symbol, carefully crafted, resembled the asterisks of the zodiac signs we were born under—a Cancer for my sister, a Libra for my younger sister, a Taurus for myself, and a Sagittarius for my brother. Even the symbol of Taurus, representing her own sign, was meticulously depicted, accompanied by another bull, symbolizing me, born on May 20th, just a few days after her birthday on May 16th.

Pieces of Me

As I think back about my mom, I want to share about my mother's bangles. They played a significant role in her life as well. She wore them every day, never taking them off. These sterling silver bangles were heavy-duty and cherished, each with its unique design: one was a fist, another a snake, and yet another an arrow. These bangles, with their rich history, were a part of her identity in the '60s and '70s. They held meaningful moments and symbolized the strength and continuity of our family. They were so significant to me, that you may have noticed I included them on the cover of this book because of their meaning.

Let me also tell you about my mother's house—it was more than just a home; it was a canvas painted with her unique passions and quirks. From the moment you stepped inside, you could sense her presence in every carefully chosen decor piece. But what truly made her house stand out were her beloved Siamese and Persian cats, Fifi and Pepe. They weren't just pets; they were guardians of the household, gracefully prowling through the halls as if they owned the place.

You see, my mother had this remarkable way of keeping her home impeccable and neat despite the presence of her furry companions. You'd never guess she had cats at all. Fifi, with her elegant Siamese features, had a special knack for finding the highest vantage points, keeping a watchful eye over everything that went on. It was as if she took her role as the house sentinel quite seriously.

And then there was Pepe, the Persian charmer, with his luxurious fur and laid-back demeanor. He had this way of melting into the background, effortlessly blending in with the plush furnishings of the house. But don't be fooled by his relaxed exterior; Pepe was just as vigilant as Fifi when it came to guarding their domain.

Together, they added an extra layer of warmth and character to our home, a testament to my mother's deep love for her feline companions. Each day was filled with their playful antics and quiet moments of companionship, reminding us that a house is more than just walls and furniture—it's a sanctuary filled with love and laughter, thanks to those who call it home.

In the midst of this enchanting atmosphere, the living room stood as a forbidden sanctuary, exclusively reserved for the grown-ups. Its door remained closed to us children, a barrier between the world of adults and our own. While the rest of the house echoed with our laughter and play, the living room remained a silent mystery, its secrets hidden behind ornate curtains and polished wooden doors. It was a room bathed in light, with glass panels spanning its walls, offering glimpses of the world within. I remember stealing glances through the crack in the door, my curiosity sparked by the faint sounds of muffled conversations drifting out from within. It was a space where older adults would gather for evenings of lively conversation and spirited debates, their laughter mingling with the clink of glasses and the music of all the old school RnB legends like Tammy Terrell, Marvin Gaye, and the Isley Brothers.

Despite our best efforts, my siblings and I were never allowed entry into that hallowed space. It was a rule we begrudgingly accepted, knowing that the living room was reserved for a different kind of entertainment, one that belonged to the world of grown-ups.

But even as we played in the other rooms, our imaginations would wander to the mysteries that lay beyond that closed door. We would dream of the day when we too would be old enough to step into that forbidden realm, to join the adults in their gatherings and become part of the stories whispered within those elegant walls. However, there was always an undeniable vibe whenever my mother threw us birthday parties. Even with the spacious basement, it inevitably transformed into an adult affair. Those were the days of growing up in the heart of New York City, immersed in the vibrant culture of the '60s and '70s. Being in an African American household encapsulated the diversity of the world I lived in—where Afro hairstyles, bell-bottom pants, miniskirts, and boots were the norm. It was an era where secrets were kept, whether for good or bad, against the backdrop of my mother's exceptional talent for entertaining friends and family.

In the midst of it all, my mother remained a loving and nurturing presence, shaping our lives with her thoughtful gestures and unique approach to the world around us. Our home on Linden Boulevard was not just a house; it was a sanctuary filled with the warmth of her love and the echoes of her curiosity. Even during our time on Waverly Avenue, her nurturing spirit prevailed, as she carried my younger sister in her womb, five months pregnant with new life.

Life in Brooklyn on Linden Blvd. was filled with battles, particularly with one of the brothers, my mother married. Amid the constant fighting, my mother bore the weight of caring for three other children from his previous relationships, forging a blended family amongst the chaos. Yet, beneath the surface of blended bonds lay the scars of abuse, a harsh reminder of the complexities that defined our existence.

While pondering the cosmos, there stood a constant figure—a faithful companion, a Doberman Pinscher, who shared our home. Yet, a darker truth lay behind the playful tunes of a trumpet, and the Doberman's harmonious howls. I recall the moments of violence, the sharp sting of a hand striking fur, a scene etched into my memory alongside the notes of a somber tune played by my mother's husband. He was the one to lay hands on the dog, tarnishing the otherwise serene atmosphere of our home.

There were times when family members had to come over due to his violent behavior, as the abuse escalated beyond control. They would intervene because it started to get out of hand. Feisty as my mother was, she wasn't going to allow a man to keep putting his hands on her. It was time she would also call her brothers for protection.

Even as our lives appeared to revolve around mysterious heavenly wonders, there were earthly struggles that cast shadows upon our existence as if dimming the very light of our day. During this time, my mother, married to her high school sweetheart, embarked on a new chapter in Lowell, MA, where she ventured into a Plastic Factory Business with one of the brothers she married. However, behind the exterior of business success lay the specter of abuse, a haunting presence that followed us like a shadow. I can still feel the tension in the air as we contemplated fleeing to another state, seeking refuge from the turmoil that plagued our lives, thinking things were going to change in behaviors; my mother still held her own.

This business was a family endeavor involving brothers, but during that time, my mother also provided funding as she came into some money after my younger sister, Reign's, father passed away. She rekindled a relationship with one of Harrington's brothers during this period of being married to this person, thinking that things would last forever and starting a new beginning in another state. Even in the face of the allure of a fresh start, the darkness of abuse and turmoil persisted, threatening to overshadow any glimmer of hope for a brighter future.

Affirmation: "I honor my roots and the strength of those who came before me."

Bible Scripture: "The LORD is my light and my salvation—whom shall, I fear? The LORD is the stronghold of my life—of whom shall I be afraid?" - Psalm 27:1 (NIV)

> **MY PAST EXPERIENCES HAVE SHAPED ME INTO A STRONGER PERSON.**

_____

_____

_____

_____

_____

_____

_____

_____

PIECES OF ME

Pieces of Me

PIECES OF ME

Chapter 3: A Sanctuary in the Shadows

As I reminisced about my childhood on Sterling Place in Brooklyn, NY, a collage of memories unfolded, revealing the joys and sorrows of my upbringing. My family found a place to call home in the bustling neighborhood of Flatbush nestled between the brownstone buildings that lined the streets. Yet, within the confines of our rented space, shadows marred childhood innocence.

During those formative years, my mother, burdened with the responsibility of providing for our family, often entrusted me with the care of a babysitter. Within the walls of that temporary refuge, I encountered experiences far beyond my tender years. The details are etched into my memory with painful clarity, a testament to the innocence lost in the face of betrayal.

The babysitter meant to safeguard our well-being, became a source of anguish and confusion as she subjected me to acts no child should endure. The weight of those moments bore down on my young shoulders, leaving scars that would remain hidden from the world for years to come.

In the midst of this turmoil, our home became a sanctuary despite the shadows of the past. Within the trials of being a child, the Kelly's, our landlords, and my oldest sister Lorraine's godparents, provided a pillar of stability and kindness. Their presence offered a respite from the darkness, a reminder that within the chaos, there were still rays of light.

Reflecting on those early years, I am reminded of the resilience that carried me through the darkest moments. Though the road was filled with challenges, I emerged from the crucible of adversity, strengthened by the trials of my early childhood.

Affirmation: "In the darkest moments, I find the strength to endure and rise above."

Bible Scripture: "The light shines in the darkness, and the darkness has not overcome it." — John 1:5 (NIV)

Pieces of Me

> I EMBRACE MY JOURNEY AND HONOR MY GROWTH.

_____

_____

_____

_____

_____

_____

_____

_____

_____

PIECES OF ME

PIECES OF ME

Chapter 4: Unveiling Truths: A Journey from Shadows to Light

I want to share the story of a young girl forced to assume full responsibility for her life journey at the tender age of ten. When my mother married her high school sweetheart, we moved from the bustling city of New York to the quiet town of Lowell, MA. However, their marriage eventually hit a rocky patch, and they ended up getting a divorce.

Reflecting on my past, I am reminded of the complexities surrounding my paternity. Theodore Mitchell Sr., the man listed on my birth certificate, was more a legal formality than a biological reality. Throughout the legal entanglements of my mother's marriage, the truth of my parentage remained obscured. For years, I held onto the belief that Raymond, a prominent figure in our family, was my father. Yet, it wasn't until a transformative conversation with my mother on the cusp of my 18th birthday year that the truth began to unravel. During a discussion in the car by the water, parked along Pawtucket Blvd in Lowell, Massachusetts, she gently disclosed the reality of my parentage, revealing Danny as my biological father. After enjoying some ice cream, we headed back to her vibrant red Camaro, its "T" shaped hood gleaming under the warm sunlight. As we settled into the car, my mother grew emotional. She turned to me, her eyes glistening with unshed tears, and began to speak with a quiver in her voice. She said she had her reasons for what she was about to share and felt it was time for me to know the truth about him and their past together. With every word, the weight of her emotions grew heavier, and soon we were both in tears, the car a small sanctuary for our shared sorrow. Through her sobs, she detailed the events and feelings that had transpired between them, ensuring I understood who he was and why things had happened the way they did. It was a heart-wrenching yet healing conversation that brought us closer together as we sat there, enveloped in the rawness of our emotions.

The revelation of my true lineage was not without its turmoil. Tensions between my brother and mother, filled with emotion and urgency, often erupted into heated exchanges. My brother's impassioned pleas to uncover the truth echoed through the walls of our home, casting a shadow of uncertainty over my identity. In their lives, Theodore Mitchell Sr.'s presence was overshadowed by his struggles with drugs, which eventually led my mother to make the difficult decision to leave him and seek a better life for herself and her children, eventually getting a divorce.

With each word, she peeled back the layers of her past, revealing how she met Danny, my biological father. Their love was passionate and consuming but also laden with challenges. My mother found herself drawn to a man whose life was deeply intertwined with the streets of New York City and whose allure was as intoxicating as it was dangerous.

As she recounted the events that led to my conception, I listened intently, hanging onto every word. She spoke of her reluctance to heed her friends' warnings, her longing to escape the confines of the Red Hook projects, and her decision to take a leap of faith and follow her heart.

Beneath the surface of her words lay a more profound truth, a truth that spoke to the complexities of love, sacrifice, and resilience. My mother's story was not just about the man she loved or the circumstances that brought them together; it was about the strength of the human spirit, the power of forgiveness, and the enduring bonds that tie us to our past.

As I reflect on that fateful day, I realize that my journey to uncover the truth about my father was also a journey to find the truth about myself. It was a journey of uncertainty, doubt, clarity, and revelation. Though the road ahead may be filled with challenges, I am filled with hope and determination, knowing that the truth has set me free to embrace the future with open arms.

Affirmation: "I am resilient and courageous, embracing the truths of my past to build a brighter future."

Bible Scripture: "For I know the plans I have for you," declares the LORD, "plans to prosper you and not to harm you, plans to give you hope and a future." - Jeremiah 29:11 (NIV)

> **I AM WORTHY OF LOVE, RESPECT, AND HAPPINESS.**

_____

_____

_____

_____

_____

_____

_____

_____

PIECES OF ME

Pieces of Me

PIECES OF ME

Chapter 5: Betrayal and Bravery: Navigating Love and Loss in 1960s Brooklyn

In the heart of Park Slope, St. James Place, and Fulton, Classon Avenue, my parents' lives unfolded against the backdrop of 1960s Brooklyn. For my mother, the vibrant club scene intertwined with her relationship with Danny, but it soon took a challenging turn. Despite her deep affection, whispers of Danny's infidelity and deceit grew louder, piercing through the love she held for him. The final straw came when she encountered other women proudly flaunting her own clothes—items Danny had taken from her closet, stark symbols of betrayal that cut deep against the values she cherished.

As the cherished daughter in her family, my mother had been doted on by her father, who admired her impeccable style and regularly showered her with new garments. These gestures only amplified her reputation as a fashion-forward figure on Brooklyn's bustling streets, making Danny's actions all the more devastating. Faced with unbearable heartache, she knew she had to make the agonizing choice to walk away, closing the chapter on those neighborhoods and bravely stepping into a new phase of her life.

As my mother faced the stark reality of her situation, life threw her a curveball when she discovered she was pregnant. Summoning every ounce of courage she had, she decided to confront Danny, the father of her unborn child.

They arranged to meet at the record store, a familiar haunt where they often crossed paths. The atmosphere crackled with tension as they exchanged words, emotions running high as my mother disclosed her pregnancy. The record store, a family-owned business known as D&D Records, held significance beyond its storefront. It was where my grandmother resided, and my father spent much of his time. My grandmother, a constant presence in the store, often retreated to an apartment upstairs. Surrounded by the vinyl records and familiar surroundings, my parents' conversation was intense. Alongside Danny's grandfather, my great-grandfather, affectionately known as Pops, my mother navigated the complexities of her situation within the familiar walls of the record store.

In the disarray, my mother contemplated the unthinkable: abortion. Considering Danny's lifestyle, bringing a child into disarray and uncertainty seemed unbearable. However, her upbringing instilled a strong sense of morality and integrity, leading her to ultimately carry me to term. The challenges continued. Upon hearing of Danny's influence in our lives, my mother's best friend Teresa expressed her concerns to my mother, urging her to distance herself from him. My mother, deeply disappointed by the revelations about Danny's character, found comfort in her faith and upbringing, emphasizing honesty, integrity, and moral living. It wasn't until years later that I learned about my biological dad, Danny.

Affirmation: "I am strong and capable, turning life's betrayals into steppingstones toward a brighter future."

Pieces of Me

Bible Scripture: "The LORD is close to the brokenhearted and saves those who are crushed in spirit." - Psalm 34:18 (NIV)

I LEARN FROM MY MISTAKES AND USE THEM TO PROPEL ME FORWARD.

_____

_____

_____

_____

_____

_____

_____

_____

_____

_____

PIECES OF ME

Pieces of Me

_____

_____

_____

_____

_____

_____

_____

_____

_____

_____

_____

_____

_____

PIECES OF ME

Chapter 6: Pillars of Strength: Love and Loss in the Shadow of Uncertainty

Having walked away from three or four years of life and love with Danny, my mother met Raymond when she was pregnant with me, and he was in the delivery room when I was born. At the heart of the anticipation of my arrival, Raymond stood tall as my mother's rock. When the day finally arrived, he didn't falter. In the delivery room, as the labor pains wracked her body, he was there, his steady presence a comforting anchor during the storm. With each sharp pang, he stood by her side, guiding her through the ordeal until we reached the hospital, where I would take my first breath, welcomed into the world by Raymond's constant support.

Raymond was an integral part of my early life, being with us for three formative years. For years, he assumed my father's role, offering steady commitment and love and support to our family. In my adolescent years, I embraced him as the only father figure I knew, never questioning his presence or significance in our lives because I was too young to understand the difference or what it meant to have a father.

During this intense time, my mother became pregnant with my sister Reign. Raymond, my younger sister, Reign's, father, emerged as a pillar of strength and stability in our lives. Unfortunately, Raymond couldn't be there for her delivery. Tragically, he was murdered, leaving us all devastated.

Raymond's life was cut short by a senseless act of violence, leaving behind a void that echoed through our family. His sudden absence shattered the sense of security we had come to rely on, and the circumstances surrounding his death remained a mystery, known only to a select few, including my uncle. The pain of his loss was compounded by the unanswered questions and the feeling of injustice that lingered in our hearts.

My uncle, who was in law enforcement, advised my mother to let it go, saying it wasn't in her best interest to investigate what happened. So, when my mother was five months pregnant, she wasn't able to attend the funeral due to circumstances involving the other side of the family. It was a very complicated situation that prevented her from being there to pay her respects.

As my journey has unfolded, his memory has remained a guiding light, illuminating the path forward as I navigate the twists and turns of my own story.

In the tapestry of my family's history, there exists a tangled thread that weaves through the fabric of my existence. Despite another man's name etched onto my birth certificate, it was Raymond who stood as a pillar of strength in the delivery room, cradling me in his arms as if I were his own flesh and blood. His presence in those early moments of my life shaped the foundation of our bond, a bond forged in the crucible of love and shared experience.

Pieces of Me

Yet, beneath the warmth of his embrace, a shadow loomed over the truth of my origins. The revelation of my father's supposed demise casted a veil of uncertainty over my identity, leaving behind fragments of memories whispered by my mother. As the chapters of my life have unfolded, the echoes of her storytelling remained, serving as guideposts in my journey of self-discovery throughout the mystery of my family's past.

Affirmation: "I honor the love and strength of those who shaped me, embracing their legacy as I forge my path forward."

Bible Scripture: "So do not fear, for I am with you; do not be dismayed, for I am your God. I will strengthen you and help you; I will uphold you with my righteous right hand." - Isaiah 41:10 (NIV)

> **I AM AT PEACE WITH MY PAST AND EXCITED FOR MY FUTURE.**

―――――――――――――――――――――――
―――――――――――――――――――――――
―――――――――――――――――――――――
―――――――――――――――――――――――
―――――――――――――――――――――――
―――――――――――――――――――――――
―――――――――――――――――――――――
―――――――――――――――――――――――
―――――――――――――――――――――――

PIECES OF ME

Pieces of Me

PIECES OF ME

Chapter 7: A Father's Love: Embracing Bonds Beyond Blood

As that fateful day dawned, marked by the turning of the calendar to May 20th, the significance of the date resonated deeply within my family's narrative. Born just after the stroke of midnight, a mere four days before my mother's own birthday, I entered the world with a quiet determination, a symbol of new beginnings and intertwined destinies. With a shock of black hair and deep brown eyes, I made my debut, weighing in at a delicate six pounds and three ounces, a tiny bundle of potential wrapped in the embrace of the early morning light.

As I mentioned in the last chapter, there I was, a newborn babe, cradled in the arms of a man who wasn't my biological father but whose love knew no bounds. As he stood before me, ensuring that my mother was well taken care of, his presence radiated strength and tireless commitment. He became a pillar of support not just for my mother, but for my siblings and me as well. This was just the beginning of the deep love that he shared with my mother, a bond that would weather the storms of life and stand the test of time. Raymond understood the complexities of the situation regarding my biological father, but it didn't matter to him. He made sure things were what they needed to be for my mother, offering his love and support unconditionally.

The stories my mother used to share about Raymond painted a vivid picture of the man who had become my father in every sense of the word. From the early days of my childhood, she recounted how Raymond would pick me up from daycare, his presence a comforting constant in my young life. I still remember the joy of clutching a bundle of bananas in my hand, a simple gesture of love from him that brought immense happiness. Everywhere he went, I was by his side, embraced by his family as if I were one of their own. Jeanette, his beloved relative, became not only a cherished family member but also my godmother. Along with the rest of his relatives, she welcomed me with open arms, showering me with love and acceptance. During those years, Peaches was another cornerstone of my early life, caring for me while my mother worked. Despite not residing with Raymond after our move to Sterling Place due to his untimely death, his family, including Peaches, continued to play a significant role in my upbringing, providing care and nurturing support in my formative years. In their eyes, I wasn't just a child of uncertain parentage; I was Raymond's child, loved and cherished without reservation. And so, I never questioned my place in their hearts, for Raymond had taken me in as his own flesh and blood, and that was all that mattered. As I reflect on these memories, they form the foundation of my life's story, a tale of love, acceptance, and belonging that I carry with me as I share my journey in this documentary of my life.

Little did I realize then that the truth of my parentage would remain shrouded in mystery until the day my mother shared her story with me, revealing Danny as my biological father. It was a revelation that shook the foundation of my identity, challenging everything I thought I knew about myself and my family. But it was also a revelation that brought clarity and understanding, paving the way for a deeper exploration of my past and a greater appreciation for the complexities of human relationships.

Affirmation: "I am grateful for the love that surrounds me, knowing that family is defined by more than just blood."

Bible Scripture: "A father to the fatherless, a defender of widows, is God in his holy dwelling. God sets the lonely in families, he leads out the prisoners with singing; but the rebellious live in a sun-scorched land." - Psalm 68:5-6 (NIV)

"I TRUST THE PROCESS OF LIFE AND MY ABILITY TO NAVIGATE IT."

_____

_____

_____

_____

_____

_____

_____

_____

PIECES OF ME

Pieces of Me

PIECES OF ME

Chapter 8: Echoes of Love and Resilience: A Brooklyn Beginning

As my mother embarked on her new life, navigating through challenges and seeking love, her connection to the Mitchell family remained strong, anchored by her marriage to Theodore Mitchell Sr. Despite the complexities of our family dynamics, their consistent love and support provided stability in our lives. My older siblings, Lorraine and Theodore Mitchell Jr., known affectionately as Moochie, played integral roles in this family fabric. Their grandmother, whom I came to regard as my own, warmly embraced me into their fold, weaving me into the texture of their lives. Despite the changes that came with moving away from New York City and marrying into the Harrington family after losing Raymond tragically, my mother maintained a strong bond with the Mitchell's.

During her time in Massachusetts, where she settled into her own apartment, my mother faced the challenge of learning to drive. In New York City, she had always relied on public transportation. Marrying into the Harrington family necessitated a new skill: driving. Determined, she obtained her learner's permit and bought a light blue Monte Carlo from the '70s, practicing tirelessly to master the art of driving.

I can still hear us shouting, "Mommy, get off the sidewalk!" as she hugged the curb during her early driving days. Her response was always the same: "Shut up, y'all, I am driving!" Despite our teasing, we couldn't help but admire her determination. With each trip to the store or weekend drive, she honed her skills, gradually becoming a confident driver. We often made weekend trips back to New York City, where she eagerly explored the city and visited family, seizing every opportunity to enrich our lives with new experiences.

Our apartment at 977 Westford Street, Lowell, Massachusetts became a sanctuary, a place where my mother's love and dedication filled every corner. And as she navigated the complexities of parenthood, her strength and resilience shone through, a guiding light in our lives in the face of the uncertainties of adolescence. This vehicle was more than just a mode of transport; it symbolized freedom and autonomy following her separation from a relationship that no longer served her. She was learning to navigate the roads and the complexities of life as a single parent. Our trips in the new car, often to the store, were adventures filled with laughter and the occasional jolt as she became proficient behind the wheel.

This car also enabled us to maintain a vital connection with our family in New York, making the three-to-four hour journey an integral part of our lives. She was especially close to her cousin, Phyllis, and cherished the moments spent with her and other relatives. My mother made sure to take us to see our grandparents, creating cherished memories and strengthening family bonds with each visit. My mother embodied the Taurus spirit—resolute, loyal, and unyielding dedication to her family. Her love was a fortress, within its walls. It is where we learned the true meaning of resilience, protection, and enduring courage.

As I explore further into my narrative, the intertwining threads of our family connections become more pronounced. My mother's niece, Annette, through marriage, later joined us and became an integral part of our household, further cementing the bond between our families. These formative years, filled with memories both cherished and challenging, laid the groundwork for the journey that lay ahead. As I embark on further discussions, I unravel the intricacies of my past and explore how these early experiences shaped the person I am today.

During those formative years, our lives unfolded within the walls of the 977 Westford Street Apartments, a place symbolic of our family's financial struggles and resilience. My mother, the unflagging pillar of our household, worked tirelessly to ensure our basic needs were met, often stretching every dollar to its limit. To aid in managing the household and its myriad demands, my mother welcomed Annette, my older brother and older sister's cousin, into our home. Annette's presence brought much-needed support, bravely lightening my mother's burden. In 1975, Annette and my mother found themselves in parallel paths as they both worked for ITEK INCORPORATED. Day in and day out, they shared the same shift, navigating the challenges of the workplace together. However, fate dealt a harsh blow when my mother was laid off, abruptly altering the course of her career. Two weeks later, in the same year, Annette faced the same fate, leaving them both grappling with uncertainty about their futures. Despite the setbacks, they leaned on each other for support, drawing strength from their shared experiences.

Affirmation: "I am resilient and strong, facing every challenge with love and determination, knowing my family's support is my foundation."

Bible Scripture: "Trust in the Lord with all your heart and lean not on your own understanding; in all your ways submit to him, and he will make your paths straight." Proverbs 3:5-6 (NIV)

Pieces of Me

> "I AM GRATEFUL FOR THE SUPPORT AND LOVE I RECEIVE."

_____

_____

_____

_____

_____

_____

_____

_____

_____

_____

PIECES OF ME

Regina Hall

_____

_____

_____

_____

_____

_____

_____

_____

_____

_____

_____

PIECES OF ME

Chapter 9: Enduring Love and Resilience: Navigating New Beginnings

During that same year, as Lorraine departed, Moochie remained behind to care for us while my mother diligently worked to support our family. Meanwhile, in the midst of 1975, Lorraine's feelings toward Massachusetts were lukewarm at best, prompting her to secretly return to New York City. Her spontaneous actions injected an element of excitement and unpredictability into our lives, keeping us constantly alert.

As for Moochie, my older brother, he yearned to leave Massachusetts, yet his deep sense of responsibility toward me and my younger sister, Reign, anchored him in place. Despite his personal aspirations, he selflessly shouldered the responsibility of caregiving during the upheaval, embodying the essence of selfless sacrifice and devoted dedication. At the time, Reign was four years old, and I was seven.

During our time in Massachusetts, my siblings' discontent with the new surroundings became increasingly evident. They longed to return to the familiar streets of New York, where the rhythm of life resonated more deeply with their hearts. Annette's frequent trips back and forth to New York mirrored their desire for a return to what they knew well. The stark absence of people of color in Massachusetts was a jarring contrast to the diverse streets they were accustomed to, amplifying their sense of displacement.

Lorraine sought comfort with our grandmother on my mother's side during this challenging period, finding comfort in the familiarity of family ties.

Meanwhile, my brother's struggles in school compounded the challenges we faced. His inability to connect with his peers often led to clashes, resulting in suspensions and added stress for our family. Being among the few Black African Americans in his school presented its own set of difficulties, as he navigated a landscape where he felt like an outsider. These were undeniably tough times for my siblings, marked by a longing for home and a struggle to find their place in a new and unfamiliar environment.

During these times, I was merely seven years old, yet the memories remain etched in my mind with vivid clarity, like scenes from a movie playing on repeat. I recall watching as my mother navigated the challenges of caring for her children surrounded by the turmoil. The struggles of my older siblings, who strongly opposed our move to Massachusetts, weighed heavily on our family.

Despite the obstacles we encountered, our connections with the Harrington's remained steadfast, providing stability through the ups and downs. We continued to refer to each other as cousins, aunts, and uncles, and our homes have remained open to one another. Even during the drama and abuse within their marriage, we stayed united as family. Though their marriage did not last long, and they eventually separated and divorced, our family bond endured.

Pieces of Me

We maintained close relationships with each other, with me often spending nights at my aunt's house, where the dynamics of children mirrored my own family's—three girls and a boy. Our commitment to one another remained unshakable, regardless of the trials we faced.

Despite the scarcity that marked those days, my mother's ingenuity and love ensured that we never felt deprived, especially during Christmas. With limited resources, she welcomed our community's generosity, transforming second-hand gifts into treasures wrapped in mystery beneath a blanket. One Christmas stands out vividly in my memory, marking a rare moment of childhood delight despite our usual hardships. That year, my mother, a member of a program designed to aid low-income families, received a gift that brought unexpected joy to my younger sister and me. It was a wooden table and chair set—a simple yet profound token of generosity from strangers who donated to families like ours during the festive season.

This modest set became more than just furniture; it was a symbol of kindness and a source of hope. We used it for everything—from eating our meals and playing games to drawing and studying. Each time I sat at that table, I felt a sense of normalcy and gratitude. The kindness of those who had never met us, yet extended their support, instilled in me an enduring belief in the goodness of others.

This gift was not just a practical aid; it was a reminder that we were not alone in our struggles. It represented the community's collective effort to lift each other up during times of need, echoing the resilience and solidarity that I came to appreciate deeply as I grew older. She carefully cleaned and polished it until it gleamed, placing it in her bedroom as a surprise for us. Alongside these, she would also go out and get other gifts, waiting to surprise us on Christmas morning. The joy and excitement of unwrapping those gifts remain etched in my memory, a testament to my mother's resourcefulness and unshakable love during challenging times. While navigating these challenges, my mother found companionship with Gary, a police officer residing within our apartment complex. He was a figure of kindness in our lives, though his presence, like a fleeting shadow, eventually faded from our story.

My mother, standing just 5 feet 2 inches tall, was a formidable force, fiercely protective of her children. Her resolve was unbreakable, and her spirit indomitable, particularly in adversity.

As I reflect on my childhood memories, one incident stands out vividly in my mind like a scene from a movie. It was a day much like any other as my mother returned home from a long day at work, weary but determined. Little did she know, her evening would take an unexpected turn before she even had the chance to step foot inside our house.

When my mom's car pulled up outside our building in Lowell, Massachusetts, she spotted the woman—a menacing figure lurking in the shadows, ready to cause trouble. And let me tell you, back then, racism was rampant, especially against African Americans like us. But my mom? She's from NYC, and she's got that no-nonsense attitude. So, without

Pieces of Me

a moment's hesitation, she jumped out of the car, her heels clicking against the pavement with purpose. In that fleeting moment, as the light of dusk faded, my mother stood tall and determined—a symbol of strength in the face of adversity. With a swift and decisive motion, she confronted the woman directly, her determination filling the air, demonstrating her strong resolve and asserting her presence unmistakably. And that lady? She didn't know what hit her!

It was a testament to my mother's unfaltering love and protection for her children, a display of courage that would forever be etched into our family's history. As the echoes of the confrontation faded into the ether, a sense of calm descended upon the once tumultuous scene, leaving a newfound appreciation for the strength and resilience that bound us together as a family.

I remember one incident vividly—it was during laundry time, and my brother, always full of mischief, decided to play a prank on me. He pretended there was a ghost outside and would dart out the back door, urging me to follow, only to leave me alone, terrified and screaming, when he ran off. On this particular occasion, as I chased after him in fear, I tripped and fell, blood trickling from my face, turning a simple prank into a frightening ordeal. My brother's antics knew no bounds, and as I lay there in pain and distress, he eventually had to bring me upstairs to show my mother the result of his horseplay. I remember the shock and concern on her face as she saw the blood all over me, and the turmoil that ensued as we dealt with the aftermath. It was a moment that etched itself into our family history, a reminder of the mischief and commotion my brother could conjure up with his imaginative scenarios. And during it all, despite the disorder he caused, he was always there, trying to make things right in his own mischievous way. The healing process of the scabs seemed to take forever, a constant reminder of that chaotic yet unforgettable day.

Another incident involved my brother's frustration when he wanted to watch a game on the floor model TV, but I didn't share his enthusiasm. In his annoyance, he pushed me, causing me to stumble and collide with a metal decor piece my mother had recently acquired. It was a man-shaped horse holding a bow and arrow, and it hadn't been properly secured to the wall. The sharp edges of the metal piece pierced my arm, leaving a deep cut that required stitches. My mother, who was in the back room, heard my cries and rushed to help, adding to the chaos of the situation.

As my brother's cooking skills blossomed during his teenage years, showcasing remarkable independence and a knack for learning, my mother played a pivotal role in nurturing his potential. Recognizing his aptitude and eager to instill independence in her only son, she took the time to teach him the ins and outs of running a household. From cooking nutritious meals to managing chores and responsibilities, my brother embraced these lessons with enthusiasm, showing a genuine passion for cooking.

As he refined his cooking abilities, it became evident that he possessed a natural talent and a desire to excel. Despite his young age, he approached each task with dedication, guided by my mother's wisdom and encouragement. Under her guidance, he not only mastered the art of cooking but also developed a strong sense of responsibility and self-sufficiency.

Throughout his teenage years, my brother's role in the household extended beyond just cooking. He became an invaluable source of support and assistance to my mother, easing her burdens and contributing to the smooth running of our home. His journey towards independence was not just about learning to cook; it was a testament to his resilience, determination, and dedicated commitment to his family. In the course of all of this, his playful nature and sense of humor brought joy and laughter to our home, making even the simplest moments memorable.

It was during this time that one of my sisters fell ill and required hospitalization. Due to the high fever, she developed seizures, adding another layer of challenge for my mother to navigate. Despite the hardships we faced, our family remained resilient, bound together by love and shared experiences.

As a single parent, my mother faced the daunting task of raising us on her own, with my siblings and me often left to our own devices as latchkey kids. Yet, despite the challenges, she remained adamant in her commitment to provide for us and ensure our safety.

As my siblings and I grew older, my mother arranged for my sister and me to attend daycare and after-school programs. Initially, we were under the care of a daycare provider, but soon transitioned to Community Teamwork, a daycare center that also offered programs like the Boys and Girls Club. Recognizing the challenges of being a single mother, my mother sought assistance to ensure we received proper care and support. It was during our time at daycare that my friendship with Jessica began to bloom.

However, it was at the Boys and Girls Club where our bond truly flourished. We were both part of the daycare program, spending our days engaged in activities and forging a bond that would last a lifetime. From the moment we met, there was an instant connection, and soon, Jessica became more than just a friend—she was like family. I remember the excitement of leaving daycare and rushing over to Jessica's house, where her welcoming mother would greet us with open arms. Those evenings were filled with laughter, chatter, and the comforting aroma of Chinese food wafting through the air, a tradition that became a cherished part of our friendship.

Jessica's long, black hair flowed down her back like a river, a vivid reflection of our deepening bond. As latchkey kids, Jessica and I spent countless afternoons together, and I was completely obsessed with her hair. It was so long that she could literally sit on it, and I was mesmerized by how it flowed like a river of silk. I loved to play with it, running my fingers through the thick, shiny strands that seemed to go on forever. Her hair became a symbol of everything I admired and longed for, something beautiful that I couldn't help but be drawn to. In those quiet moments after school, her hair wasn't just hair; it was a connection to a world of beauty and mystery that I wanted to be a part of.

Together, we navigated the ups and downs of childhood, inseparable companions on the journey of growing up. On Fridays, Jessica's mother would treat us to dinner at our favorite Chinese restaurant, a weekly ritual that we eagerly anticipated. I would always have my change of clothes ready, knowing that if Jessica's mother picked us up, I would be spending the night at Jessica's house, where our adventures would continue long into the evening.

Affirmation: "I am resilient and grateful for the enduring love and support of my family, which guides me through life's challenges."

Bible Scripture: "And we know that in all things God works for the good of those who love him, who have been called according to his purpose." - Romans 8:28 (NIV)

> **I AM EMPOWERED TO CREATE THE LIFE I DESIRE.**

_____

_____

_____

_____

_____

_____

_____

_____

_____

_____

Pieces of Me

_____

_____

_____

_____

_____

_____

_____

_____

_____

_____

_____

_____

_____

PIECES OF ME

Chapter 10: Bound by Love: Family, Challenges, and Unbreakable Bonds

Eventually, my mother decided to leave her apartment, and we temporarily moved in with my mom's friend, Tootsie, who had two daughters, until we could secure our own place at the Chariot Apartments. We ended up staying with her for a few months at Westminster Apartments until we could find a place to live. We all stayed there. It offered us temporary shelter despite the limited space in her house. We all slept on floor cushions in a shared room. Living with her provided a temporary reprieve from the instability we had grown accustomed to, but it also brought its own set of challenges. These changes marked a pivotal chapter in our family's story, filled with uncertainty and the unfolding of events.

With each move came a sense of anticipation, uncertainty, and promise of new beginnings. Despite the challenges of adjusting to new surroundings, my mother's resilience and determination never wavered. She faced each obstacle head-on, guided by her consistent commitment to providing a better life for our family.

During this period of transition, as we settled into our new apartment, my younger sister and I adjusted to our changed routines and surroundings with the support of community programs under my mother's guidance. We thrived, navigating the challenges of childhood with determination. Balancing parenthood and work, my mother also ventured into the complexities of the dating scene, seeking companionship and support. It was during this time that we met the man who would become a significant figure in our lives. I vividly recall the day he entered our world—a charming smile, a warm embrace that promised stability and companionship. As our bond with him grew stronger, we embarked on another transition, moving to a different apartment building.

In the backdrop of change and adaptation that the Middlesex Street Chariot Apartments represented for us, the dynamics within our family were equally complex and rich in meaning. His arrival marked a significant shift not only in our family structure but also in how we related to one another. Initially curious, my brother and sister observed Benjamin's gradual development of a relationship. He was initially involved with another person before his friendship with my mother developed into a romantic relationship.

As time passed, Benjamin's visits shifted from 977 Westford Street in Lowell to the Chariot Apartments, coinciding with our family's moves and transitions. His presence became a constant in our lives, yet the unfolding events remained cloaked in uncertainty. Each moment seemed unpredictable, leaving us unsure of what the future held. In the blink of an eye, my siblings and I found ourselves caught up in the rapid changes of life. Despite my youth, I watched with keen curiosity, sensing I was witnessing something beyond my years.

With time, Benjamin seamlessly transitioned from a visitor to a permanent, integral part of our household. The way we addressed him reflected our journey of acceptance and adaptation. While my older siblings, Lorraine and Moochie, continued to call him 'Benjamin,' acknowledging his role with mature understanding, my younger sister and I affectionately referred to him as 'Daddy.' This name symbolized the deep love and acceptance we felt for him as a father figure in our lives.

Living under Benjamin's roof brought its own set of challenges, distinctly marking a departure from what we had known. His approach to discipline was harsh, and rooted in his own upbringing, which seemed to mirror the severity of older, uncompromising generations. He imposed a strict rule that we be home before the streetlights flickered to life each evening—a rule that, when broken, had painful consequences.

I vividly recall the chilling fear that gripped me the times we failed to meet his curfew. In those moments, Benjamin would step outside to break a branch from a nearby tree, a precursor to the punishment that awaited us. The sound of the snapping wood was a stark herald of the impending pain. His method of discipline was not just a physical ordeal but an emotional trauma that left deep scars, influencing my understanding of what a father should be.

Crying out to my mother, I pleaded with her, desperate to avoid the stinging lashes of the tree branch. "Please, don't let him hit us," I would beg, but the rules under Benjamin's roof were unyielding. We would rush, hearts pounding, as the twilight deepened, but sometimes, it was just too late.

Reflecting on these memories, I recognize the profound impact that Benjamin's upbringing and beliefs about discipline had on his actions. It was a cycle of fear and pain, passed down from one generation to the next, a cycle I yearned to break as I grew to understand the difference between discipline and cruelty. Despite the fear and the pain associated with his strict discipline, I still looked to Benjamin as the father figure in my life. He was the man at the helm of our household, the one who set the rules and boundaries within which we lived. His presence was a constant in the shifting reality of my childhood, and as time passed, I learned to navigate the complexities of this relationship, understanding that he, too, was shaped by his own difficult past.

It was not just my sister, brother, and I who felt the weight of his authority—his struggles seemed to envelop him, often manifesting in mental shifts that were both puzzling and deeply concerning. I witnessed the strain in his relationship with my mother, the arguments that would escalate into altercations, disagreements over matters both trivial and significant. These moments painted a portrait of a man grappling with inner turmoil, a man far removed from the uncompromising disciplinarian I feared.

Watching him as a little girl, I developed a compassionate heart towards Benjamin. I saw the struggles etched across his face, the weariness clouding his eyes, and I felt a profound urge to understand and perhaps alleviate his burdens. This empathy did not erase the fear or the pain of the punishments, but it allowed me a glimpse into the human behind the facade, the person struggling beneath the surface. Benjamin carried with him the heavy burden of his experiences in Vietnam, often overcome by profound sadness as he remembered his mother. Witnessing his vulnerability in these moments, I, even as a young girl, offered what comfort I could with hugs and gentle reassurance, whispering, "Daddy, it's going to be okay," in an attempt to soothe the pain of his past battles.

His experiences in Vietnam also manifested in unexpected ways, such as his heightened sense of alertness and readiness for confrontation. I often observed him, seemingly waiting for an enemy, perhaps someone in the complex with whom he may have had a disagreement, to cross his path, ready to defend himself at a moment's notice. This vigilance was a stark reminder of the challenges he had faced in the past, and it occasionally led to tense situations.

One such instance was when my brother faced bullying in school. A blond-headed boy would repeatedly pick on my brother, prompting my mother to intervene. She instructed my brother to stand up for himself, warning him that if he returned home without standing up to the bully, there would be consequences. I remember my brother, attending Daley Junior High School, bravely confronting the bully, holding his own in the face of adversity.

Among the myriads of childhood memories, some of the most vivid ones involve Benjamin and our trips to the pool. It was there that I learned to swim, a skill he taught in his usual uncompromising manner. One moment stands out: Benjamin throwing me into the deep end of the pool. The shock of the cold water was immediate, but as I surfaced, gasping for air, I realized that the water was supporting me. It was a terrifying yet exhilarating moment that taught me not only how to swim but also a deeper lesson about facing and overcoming my fears.

This experience was emblematic of Benjamin's approach to life. He had a good heart and wanted to prepare us for the world in his own way, pushing us beyond our comfort zones. This method, while harsh, did strip away some of my childhood fears and instilled in me a resilience that I would carry into adulthood.

Our family wasn't isolated in these experiences; we formed connections within our community that were both supportive and chaotic. My mother grew close to a woman in our complex, while Benjamin bonded with her husband. These friendships brought us together in celebration and mutual support, but they also exposed us to the inevitable dramas that unfold in close-knit communities. The highs and lows of these relationships mirrored the complexities of our own family dynamics, teaching me valuable lessons about community, support, and the messiness of human relationships.

These challenges, both personal and external, tested our family's resilience and strengthened our bonds. Despite the racism and adversity, we encountered, especially after moving from New York City to Massachusetts, we stood united, facing each obstacle with determination and love.

Pieces of Me

Surrounded by these struggles, Benjamin found comfort and joy in his connection with my mother, particularly during their weekend outings to the Commodore Nightclub, known today as the Commodore Ballroom. These moments provided a much-needed escape, allowing them to immerse themselves in the vibrant music scene of the '70s. Benjamin was particularly fond of the music artist Al Green; he would often mimic the singer's voice, making it his own. Whenever the club hosted talent events like the "Gong Show," (similar to today's America's Got Talent) Benjamin enthusiastically participated, often practicing Al Green's songs in front of a mirror to prepare himself to win.

Meanwhile, my brother took on the responsibility of looking after me and my younger sister during these outings, his protective care never wavering despite any reluctance he may have felt. Benjamin's adoption of the California curls and his cherished navy blue 1970s Buick Riviera were more than just stylistic choices—he would often get roller sets from my mother after he washed his hair and sat under the hair dryer. They were expressions of his identity and a means to reclaim a sense of normalcy through the complexities of our family dynamics.

The interplay of these dynamics—the varied responses to Benjamin's role, his internal struggles, the moments of joy found in music and dance, and his engagement with the cultural expressions of the time—crafted a complex yet profoundly meaningful picture of our family life. These aspects, from personal struggles to moments of joy and artistic expression, contributed significantly to the rich tapestry of our shared story, highlighting the resilience, love, and nuanced understanding that bound us together through times of change.

Those early years were a mix of challenges, complexity, and moments filled with strength and love. My mother's dedicated commitment to caring for her children, supported by Benjamin and a network of individuals including church members, family, friends, and acquaintances, deeply influenced the person I am today. Their combined support and guidance were pivotal in navigating our journey, leaving a profound impact on my life.

But as we faced the world's challenges, there were still some obstacles. It was shocking that many different things took place when my mother said she was getting married, but I found out she was much older, and he wasn't honest about his age in the beginning. My siblings and I knew that another man was in our lives. It was when they dated and grew close, eventually leading to him moving in with us. This decision culminated in their marriage at the Justice of Peace on July 25th, 1976, when I was between seven and eight years old. This marked the beginning of a new chapter in our lives, with someone new entering our family circle. As events unfolded, we witnessed things we shouldn't have seen, and life began to present challenges. We watched as things unfolded before our eyes, navigating through the difficulties that arose. We had a lot of difficult moments; we were moving to different places. I remember living in a hotel in Nashua, NH, for a few weeks because of many of our financial issues. My younger sister and I were getting dropped off at school. I also remember that in May 1977, we got 20 inches of snow. And I couldn't go to school. It was

Pieces of Me

in that month of May when I was living in Massachusetts, that we had to sleep on the floor of the hotel room, cramped together but trying to make the best of it, building forts out of pillows and blankets to escape from the harsh reality of our situation, even if just for a moment.

Affirmation: "I am resilient and adaptable, finding strength in family and embracing each new chapter with courage."

Bible Scripture: "but those who hope in the LORD will renew their strength. They will soar on wings like eagles; they will run and not grow weary; they will walk and not be faint." - Isaiah 40:31 (NIV)

> "MY INNER STRENGTH IS MY GREATEST ASSET."

PIECES OF ME

Pieces of Me

PIECES OF ME

Chapter 11: Transitions and Trials: Navigating New Beginnings

My mother was going back to school to get her degree, and she finished. She started working at Raytheon, and then my father started working at Boston Railroads, but we moved to different places. Then we moved into a duplex house in the '70s on Christman Ave. in Lowell, Mass. As was mentioned in the last chapter, we also stayed with other people to get extra stability; it was very uncomfortable. Despite the challenges, a deep bond held us together—a bond forged through the trials we faced as a family. My mother, Dolores, and her strength and resilience inspired me to keep pushing forward, even when the weight of our circumstances threatened to overwhelm me. As our narrative unfolded against the backdrop of Lowell, Massachusetts, it became a tapestry rich with the hues of struggle, faith, and transformation. As I reflect back onto when Benjamin stepped into our lives, he not only merely filled the void left by time and circumstance but weaved himself into the fabric of our existence with threads of stability, love, and support.

His presence was a steady anchor for my mother in the turbulent sea of change, offering us a haven of security and warmth through the storms. It was a novel experience for Benjamin, as he didn't have any children when he entered my mother's life. However, there was a little boy from a previous relationship who briefly played a part in Benjamin's life before fading away as my mother and he became more involved with each other. This dynamic added an extra layer of complexity to our family dynamic, especially for my older siblings who were more acutely aware of the situation.

It was during those times when Benjamin's behavior turned violent and abusive towards my mother and brother. The environment became tense and unsafe, as we witnessed the distressing scenes unfold before our eyes. I vividly recall the sound of bathroom doors being knocked down as my brother tried to intervene, desperately attempting to protect our family. One of the most harrowing memories etched into my mind is the sight of my mother suffering from a fractured nose, a physical manifestation of the turmoil that brewed within our walls. The violence wasn't limited to her; my brother, in his vulnerability and desperate need to protect our mother, faced Benjamin's wrath as well. The image of him being kicked beneath the table in the chaos paints a vivid picture of the battleground our home had become.

There were also ongoing struggles with abuse, and my brother found it difficult to cope with the turmoil that surrounded us. Unable to reconcile the presence of a man in our lives with the pain he witnessed, he rebelled against authority and struggled to accept a father figure who didn't fulfill the role he yearned for. The trauma he endured made it challenging for him to perceive this figure as a true father, given the circumstances he witnessed.

Living on Christman Avenue, my sister and I faced the daily routine of walking to Riverside Elementary School. There was no school bus, so we joined a group of neighborhood kids each morning, forming a small procession through the streets. Those walks are etched in my memory, not the least because of Laddie, our miniature collie, who would often follow us to school. One distressing day, Laddie didn't return home. We arrived back to find our mother peering out the window, tears streaming down her face, hoping for Laddie's safe return. Her love for that dog was profound, and his disappearance left a void in her heart that never quite healed.

During these walks, we also faced the harsh realities of racism. Insults and cruel names were hurled at us, piercing our young hearts. But my sister and I learned to stand up for ourselves, to fight back against the bullies. I remember once, in a burst of defiance, we even pushed a tormenting boy into a lake. These experiences of adversity and resistance were formative, shaping our understanding of the world and our place within it.

On Christman Avenue, our neighbors played a significant role in our childhood. They were exceptionally welcoming to my sister and me, often coming to our door to invite us over or waiting for us to join them outside. Before I could join in the fun, however, I had responsibilities to fulfill. I would often call my mother at work to ask for permission to go across the street, but not before ensuring our home was spotless. I took pride in the cleanliness of our house, carefully washing the dishes and tidying up every room. Meanwhile, I'd let my younger sister go ahead and play, knowing I'd join her soon after my chores were done.

Summer days were a special time. The sun would bronze my skin as we played outside, creating lasting memories of laughter and freedom. Yet, even in the middle of this carefree joy, routines were maintained—like clockwork, our friends' parents would call them in for dinner at five o'clock, signaling that it was time for us to head home as well. It was then up to me to prepare our evening meal, a responsibility I took on due to our parents' demanding work schedules. They worked tirelessly to provide for us, and in my own way, by managing our home and meals, I contributed to our family's well-being.

Looking back, those days on Christman Avenue were filled with learning and growth. Not only did I learn the importance of responsibility and hard work, but I also experienced the joy of community and the warmth of neighborly kindness. These experiences enriched my childhood, teaching me valuable life skills and the significance of looking out for one another. Yet, even as children, those responsibilities loomed large. I remember rushing home to cook dinner and clean the house, tasks that fell to me from a young age. My father, who was not our biological parent, played a complex role in our lives. He taught me practical skills like making a bed and straightening hair—although not always gently. Let me explain what I mean. Among the many tasks my father took upon himself was managing our hair with a straightening comb. He was careful, always trying to shield our ears with his hands, but despite his best efforts, we often ended up with small burns behind our ears. These moments, though tinged with the discomfort of minor burns, also brought us closer, filled with laughter and his attempts to make us feel beautiful. He was not perfect, but his efforts were a testament to his care.

Cooking was another realm where his love was evident, though through his cooking experiments. He would proudly serve us spaghetti, the sauce invariably watery yet made with enthusiasm. We would assure him it was delicious, appreciating his effort, but secretly, we all looked forward to the meals prepared by my mother. Her cooking was exceptional; every dish she made was infused with skill and love, especially precious because of her demanding work schedule. When she cooked, she would prepare ample portions, often leaving us with leftovers.

These everyday experiences, from hair care mishaps to homemade dinners, formed the fabric of our family life. They were not just routine activities but moments of bonding, learning, and growing together. They showed us that love often came mixed with imperfections, and that laughter can ease discomfort. Through these small, shared trials and triumphs, we learned the depths of family love and the importance of perseverance.

My mother worked tirelessly, holding down a job at Filene's department store among her other commitments, which meant that the responsibility of caring for my sister often fell to me. I took pride in preparing meals, like chicken wings with teriyaki sauce and rice, ensuring that everything was ready when my parents came home from work.

Reflecting on those days at Christman Avenue brings to mind a particularly memorable moment when my mother decided it was time for my brother Moochie to join the military. She believed it would help him become more disciplined and responsible—essentially, her way of helping him "become a man." With determined resolve, she drove him to the recruitment office in Lowell, but something prompted her to circle around to the back of the building. To her surprise—and our amusement—there was Moochie, sneaking out the back door. He declared with unfailing certainty, "I ain't joining no military." His defiance was not just humorous but a clear statement of his determination to carve his own path, regardless of our mother's wishes.

This was not an isolated incident. Watching Moochie and my siblings over the years, I saw how each rebelled in their own way against the expectations set for them. It was tough, witnessing their struggles and the friction it caused with our mother, but these moments also revealed the strength and individuality of each. Moochie, in his own right, was determined to follow a path he chose for himself, not one laid out by anyone else. Lorraine, similarly, rebellious, always wanted to do things her own way, often clashing with the family norms. My mother had to keep a close eye on her, continually steering her back on track. Lorraine's defiance wasn't just teenage rebellion—it seemed fueled by things she and Moochie were exposed to that they perhaps shouldn't have been at such young ages. Despite this, it wasn't as if they were meant to see these things; my mother was fiercely protective of all of us.

Pieces of Me

These formative years on Christman Avenue were filled with both trials and lessons. They were a time of learning to navigate both the joys and injustices of life, of taking on responsibilities far beyond my years, and of forming the resilience and strength that would carry me forward.

Affirmation: "I am a pillar of strength and resilience, embracing each challenge as an opportunity to grow. With faith as my anchor and family as my foundation, I rise above adversity with grace and courage, becoming wiser and more compassionate with every step I take."

Bible Scripture: "I consider that our present sufferings are not worth comparing with the glory that will be revealed in us." - Romans 8:18 (NIV)

> **I FORGIVE MYSELF AND OTHERS FOR PAST TRANSGRESSIONS.**

_____

_____

_____

_____

_____

_____

_____

_____

Pieces of Me

PIECES OF ME

Chapter 12: Forged in Faith: Triumphs and Trials of Family Bonds

The crucial moment came when my mother, with a heart heavy with the past and eyes set on a brighter horizon, embraced her faith anew. I was ten when she embarked on this spiritual journey, a path that would draw our entire family into its embrace. Once echoing with the sounds of everyday life, our home began to resonate with the deeper tones of prayer and worship. But this transformation happened slowly over time, spearheaded by my mother's renewed faith, marked a significant turning point for us all, illuminating our lives with a glow of hope and unity.

Despite the shadows that lingered, like Benjamin's struggle with alcoholism, the light of faith proved more decisive, guiding him toward a moment of revelation. A simple act of companionship, an invitation from a friend he met through his work on the Boston Railroad tracks, led him to a church service that would change his life. That day at the First Church of God in Roxbury, Mass, became the cornerstone of Benjamin's spiritual awakening, inspiring him to walk a new path alongside us, his heart and soul aflame with a newfound purpose.

Our home transformed into a sanctuary where the rhythms of church life—the joyous hymns and the reflective Bible studies—became the soundtrack of our existence. These experiences, from singing in the choir to gathering around the Word, wove us closer together, binding us in a shared journey toward grace and redemption.

Yet, alongside this spiritual reawakening, life's complexities did not pause. My sister Lorraine's story unfolded as a poignant reminder of the challenges and choices that sculpted each of our paths. At just sixteen, she entered marriage, a union born of youth and circumstance. This chapter of her life, enriched by the birth of her daughter, was a testament to the intricate dance of love, commitment, and resilience in the face of adversity.

As the middle child, my perspective was one of observation and growth, my eyes open to the unfolding dramas and triumphs of my family saga. From the joy of shared worship to the solemnity of my sister Lorraine's wedding, each moment became a thread woven into the rich tapestry of my life. Witnessing Lorraine navigate the waters of marriage and motherhood against the backdrop of challenges and the strength of her spirit left an indelible mark on me, shaping my understanding of my own story.

My journey, marked by the trials of blending a family and the challenges of change, was also a journey of discovery. In embracing faith and family bonds, I found the strength to face the storms, grow, and transform. This story, rooted in the heart of Lowell, is a narrative of resilience, of love tested and reaffirmed, of a family finding its way through life's challenges toward a deeper understanding of faith, unity, and the enduring power of hope.

Pieces of Me

Among all the moments of grace, my stepfather Benjamin entered our lives as a stabilizing force. While we initially welcomed his love and support, his struggles, insecurities, and occasional outbursts of violence sometimes obscured that image, casting doubt on the stability we had hoped for. During this period, my parents attended a memorable New Year's Eve party at John and Joan's house, where they enjoyed the festivities and companionship. It was there that the idea of attending church together first took root. The invitation stemmed from a chance encounter with John at the railroad tracks, where he warmly invited my parents to join them at the First Church of God in Roxbury, Massachusetts. This experience deeply moved Benjamin, leading him to commit his heart to Christ.

Soon after, our entire household became immersed in the rhythms of church life. I fondly recall our participation in the choir, singing joyful hymns like 'I'm gonna sing, sing, sing, I'm gonna shout praise the Lord.' Saturday choir rehearsals and regular Bible studies became integral parts of our lives, shaping our understanding of Christianity and drawing us closer to God's love and grace. While living in Lowell, Mass, I vividly recall the transformative moment when my parents embraced Christianity. I was ten when my mother's journey back to her faith began. Despite growing up in a household steeped in Christian tradition, her return to the Lord as an adult marked a significant turning point for our family. I remember the evenings spent at Bible study, my mother diligently preparing my sister Reign and me for church, dressing us in our Sunday best. She worked at Filene's department store where she would get all the

87

discounts, and she took full advantage of this perk to dress us up in dresses, often making us look like twins. This attention to detail extended beyond church attire; she also ensured we were impeccably dressed for school pictures, making every moment a cherished memory captured in photographs.

Despite the fear and the danger, my brother's courage stood out. Even as a little boy, he exhibited a protectiveness and bravery far beyond his years, fighting back against the injustices inflicted upon our mother. His actions were not just about defense but about asserting a sense of safety and normalcy in a turned upside-down world. His resilience in the face of such adversity was a testament to the love and loyalty that persisted despite the turmoil.

It reached a point where my brother's struggles became too overwhelming, leading him to seek refuge in New York with my mother's cousin. Unable to endure the abuse any longer, he embarked on a new chapter of his life under the care of my mother's cousin, who welcomed him with open arms as if he were her own child. Though it was a difficult decision, my mother ultimately allowed him to go, recognizing that it was in his best interest. My brother's intelligence and resilience became apparent as he grew older, but he still felt like he didn't belong. I had to step up and take on additional responsibilities during this time.

I was between 11 to 12 years old when responsibilities began to fall heavily on my shoulders. Unlike my friends who enjoyed carefree moments of childhood, I rarely had the luxury to play. Even when I did step outside to play with my two friends across the street, I was always aware of the looming responsibilities awaiting me indoors.

While other kids my age were frolicking outdoors, I was tasked with caring for my younger sister, Reign, often sacrificing my desires for her well-being. Birthdays and special occasions were subject to my duties too. Though my mother made sure to celebrate my birthdays with sleepovers and cakes, I still had to ensure the house was tidy and everything was in order.

Despite the weight of responsibility, I cherished the moments of joy and connection with my friends, however brief they may have been. And though my childhood was marked by duties and obligations beyond my years, the love and support of my family sustained me through it all.

Growing up, the church played a central role in our lives, especially after my father devoted himself to his faith. This spiritual commitment brought our family new routines and a sense of purpose. I remember the transformative impact it had, not just on him but on all of us. He would throw himself into church activities, teaching us Bible verses, which he chalked up on a blackboard he'd gotten us one Christmas. His dedication was a profound example of a life altered by faith, exemplified the day he walked into the church, a bottle of alcohol in hand, only to leave it at the altar as he dedicated his life to God.

Reflecting on those days, I see how deeply my parents influenced our lives' path and the values we embraced. Every Sunday morning, my mother would rise early at 7 o'clock, filling our home with the aroma of her cooking as she prepared her beloved Sunday dinner, accompanied by the soulful melodies of her favorite gospel music. From Tramaine Hawkins to Walker Hawkins, she played every traditional gospel, infusing our home with the uplifting spirit of worship. Tramaine Hawkins's voice soared with 'Goin' Up Yonder,' a powerful anthem of hope and faith that stirred my mother's soul. And then there was Walter Hawkins, with his timeless song 'Be Grateful,' a reminder to count our blessings. As the music filled the air, my mother's joy was palpable, her love for gospel music evident in every note she played. Alongside the music, we would also watch Fred Price, immersing ourselves in the teachings of faith and spirituality. With each Sunday morning, my mother's devotion to her routine served as a guiding light of strength and inspiration, shaping our family's bond and instilling in us a profound appreciation for both tradition and faith.

Meanwhile, my mother celebrated each of us in her way. Every birthday was an event—sleepovers with friends, cakes from a local baker who worked at Raytheon. This woman was a skilled technician and an incredibly creative baker, and she crafted the most imaginative cakes possible. Whether they were shaped like Oreos or transformed into elaborate Barbie gowns with black Barbies, her cakes were the centerpiece of my birthday celebrations. These festive occasions were a testament to my mother's love, making each year memorable. Her cooking skills were renowned, drawing friends and church members together, especially when she cooked her famous ribs and collard greens or when we had lobsters brought in from Maine. Our home became a hub of fellowship, frequently hosting dinners that extended well into the evening, filled with laughter and shared stories.

Our regular trips to Boston for church on Sundays and Wednesdays became a staple of our routine. It was a journey we all took together, reinforcing our bond as a family and with our wider community. These experiences were not just about faith; they were about creating a supportive network: a sense of belonging that permeated every aspect of our lives.

Education was another pillar my mother insisted on. She was adamant about the quality of our schooling, preferring diverse environments she believed would offer the best educational opportunities. She invested in educational games like Speak & Spell and Simon Says, and workbooks that ensured our learning continued at home. Her philosophy was clear: our education was paramount, and nothing would hinder our academic growth.

Reflecting on these days, I see how deeply my parents influenced our life path and the values we embraced. Their actions, from the festive to the spiritual, shaped a childhood filled with learning, faith, and a profound sense of community responsibility. On Christman Avenue, our style was a statement of its own, thanks mainly to my mother's impeccable taste and her job at Filene's department store, which afforded us the luxury of designer labels at a discount. I vividly remember my first pair of Calvin Klein jeans and the stylish boots accompanying them. These early experiences with fashion were more than just about clothes;

they were about self-expression and my mother's pride in presenting us to the world.

Not only were we well-dressed, but we also kept our hair just as refined. I remember my first hair relaxer—a significant rite of passage for me, administered by Kenyetta, a hairstylist my mother trusted implicitly. Our visits to her salon in Boston were cleverly coordinated with our weekly trips to Bible study or right after my mother's workday ended, embedding our grooming rituals within our routine of faith and community.

Living on Christman Avenue intertwined these elements of fashion and faith in a complex tapestry. Our parents were deeply involved with our church, fostering a closeness with the congregation that felt like extended family. Yet, life was not without its contradictions and challenges. There were moments of backsliding, instances when the ideals of our Christian faith were tested, and not always upheld as one might expect. These experiences, though at times disheartening, taught us valuable lessons about grace and personal growth.

Reflecting on these times, it became clear how much our parents influenced our beliefs and how we presented ourselves to the world. From the stylish cut of our jeans to the verses we learned by heart, each detail was a thread in the fabric of our upbringing, woven with the values and aspirations they held dear.

Sadly, my siblings' lack of responsibility placed burdens on my shoulders far beyond my years. I vividly recall the

Pieces of Me

day my sister, just 16 years old, walked down the aisle, her belly swollen with life. It was a surreal moment, watching from the sidelines as our family's circumstances unfolded before my eyes. Seeing her exchange vows while still a child left a profound impression on me, a witness to the complexities of her situation. A mere 19-years-old, her husband seemed scarcely more than a boy. Yet, fate had intertwined our lives through our father Benjamin's connections with their family. Lorraine's tender age, and the acknowledgment of their youth, underscored the gravity of our reality. My mother, with a heavy heart but a sense of necessity, gave her reluctant permission, signing the papers that would bind them legally. As I held the train of her gown, walking down the aisle beside her, I observed a premature and poignant wedding. And so, my sister brought life into this world in October of 1978 while I watched, a silent witness to the unfolding drama of our family's trials.

On Christman Avenue, our home was a microcosm of life's broader canvas, echoing the joys and sorrows of our shared experiences. Lorraine's early marriage, thrust upon her by circumstance and swift decisions, was a chapter marked by intense emotion and significant challenges. As she navigated her new role, not just as a wife, but also as a mother at a young age, her resilience was put to the test.

The battles at home, born from distrust and youthful haste, often spilled over to our doorstep, where Lorraine sought comfort and understanding. Despite the turmoil, she found strength in her roots, often returning to the safety of our mother's house when the weight of her struggles grew too heavy. Her visits were not just escapes, but also reunions, reminding us of the bonds that held our family together through thick and thin.

The birth of my niece brought a new dimension to these dynamics. With no crib immediately available, my parents adapted a drawer into a cozy bassinet, a testament to our family's ingenuity and ability to make do with the resources at hand. This makeshift solution was more than just a place for the baby to sleep—it symbolized our adaptability and the love we could provide in even less-than-ideal circumstances.

Lorraine's feisty spirit never waned; her armor and strength helped her fiercely advocate for herself and her daughter. Though fraught with difficulty, her trials were also filled with lessons about perseverance and the power of self-respect.

As the years passed, the narrative of our lives on Christman Avenue continued to evolve, woven with the threads of personal challenge, community support, and unbreakable family ties. Each story, including Lorraine's, added depth to our collective history, teaching us invaluable lessons about the complexities of life and the enduring strength of family. I was just ten years old then, and I witnessed Lorraine's struggles as she tried to make her marriage work. I often saw disagreements between her and her husband, as she suspected him of infidelity. Since Lorraine was the oldest and already had a family, my mother frequently brought me and my sister Reign to Lorraine's house, where she would babysit us.

Pieces of Me

    I distinctly remember one occasion when my niece Sophia, then eight months old, was in her baby carrier, and my sister was visibly upset. This incident occurred at my house while my parents were out, and Lorraine and her husband began to argue. Unfortunately, her marriage did not last long, and she had to raise her child as a single mother.

    Life took an unexpected turn when my sister Lorraine faced challenges, leaving our mother, Dolores, to care for her child, Sophia—my niece. As Dolores stepped into the role of both mother and grandmother, the weight of this responsibility fell heavily on her shoulders.

    During that time, my sister had a nervous breakdown due to her husband leaving her unexpectedly. We found my sister on the kitchen floor at her house with the phone off the hook when we tried to call her. A moment of heartbreak and disbelief shook our family to its core.

    For me, it meant stepping up in ways I never imagined. At age 10, I juggled school, chores, and caring for our extended family. This included combing Sophia and Reign's hair and ensuring everyone's needs were met. Weekends became synonymous with trips to the laundromat, where I ensured everyone had clothes that were clean and ready for the week ahead. Facing these challenges, I took on the caretaker responsibilities with a sense of duty and love. Cooking meals, cleaning the house, and ensuring my sister Reign and my niece Sophia took their baths before bed became routine tasks for me. Tucking them in at night, providing a sense of security and warmth, was a role I embraced wholeheartedly throughout the chaos of our lives. My mother worked two jobs then, and my parents were often not home because they were trying to provide for us. As a result, I had to take on the responsibility of caring for everyone. Despite the weight of these responsibilities, I learned to clean a house like an adult, as my parents relied heavily on me.

Looking back, those years were filled with hardship but were also a testament to the power of love and family. We may have faced adversity but emerged more robust, united by a bond that could weather any storm. And though the road was tough, it was filled with moments of joy and triumph, reminding us that love is the most significant force.

While a place of love and shared history, our household also harbored intense struggles that deeply marked our lives. Benjamin, who stood as a father figure to me and my siblings, battled with alcoholism—a struggle that cast long shadows over our family life. This battle with addiction often led to fighting and instances of abuse, casting a pall over what should have been a sanctuary for us.

The violence unfolded with a chilling regularity; its beginnings traceable to our time on Christman Ave. in South Lowell. It was there that acts of violence shattered the tranquility of our home—Benjamin laying hands on my mother, Dolores, in moments that seemed to freeze time, leaving scars that were not just physical but deeply emotional. Witnessing the person who was supposed to be a pillar of strength and protection for our family become the source of fear and pain. It was a stark contradiction that I grappled with from a young age.

These experiences, as harsh and painful as they were, played a significant role in shaping my perception of relationships and family dynamics. The contrast between the love that bound us as a family and the violence that threatened to tear us apart was a complex reality that I navigated from a young age. It taught me about the duality of human nature, the capacity for both tenderness and violence and the resilience needed to forge a path forward in the aftermath of such turmoil. However, as time passed, a glimmer of hope emerged as my parents started attending church.

What I didn't share earlier is that Initially it was my mother who immersed herself in church activities, attending Bible studies and seeking comfort in the teachings of faith. This dedication often led to tension with my father, who accused her of being too involved with the pastor. Yet, despite the discord, a significant change occurred when my father decided to turn his life around.

Through the twists and turns of our journey, I learned valuable lessons about strength, resilience, and the power of faith. Despite our hardships, my parents' determined commitment to creating a better life for us prevailed. Their efforts culminated in purchasing a home, a symbol of stability and security for our family.

Affirmation: "I am strong and resilient, finding strength in my family's love and my faith, facing every challenge with courage and hope."

Bible Scripture: "Not only so, but we also glory in our sufferings, because we know that suffering produces perseverance; perseverance, character; and character, hope. And hope does not put us to shame, because God's love has been poured out into our hearts through the Holy Spirit, who has been given to us." - Romans 5:3-5 (NIV)

Pieces of Me

> "I AM OPEN TO NEW OPPORTUNITIES AND EXPERIENCES."

PIECES OF ME

PIECES OF ME

Chapter 13: Resilience and Redemption: A Journey of Hope and Healing

We found a single-family home rental in Chelmsford, Massachusetts, before my parents discovered a house on El Dorado Road. Fate intervened when the landlord owners decided to sell the property to my parents, prompting my grandfather to offer his support by lending my mother the money for our first house. My mother's resilience and determination, evident to my grandfather, were the driving force behind his belief in her ability to stabilize our family. With his backing, we finally found the permanence and security we had longed for, allowing us to flourish in our new home.

During my childhood, I spent summers as a little girl, starting at 12-years-old, visiting my grandparents and staying with them because, due to my numerous responsibilities, they felt like I needed time away. They came up with the idea of me spending every summer with them, and during those summers, I also cared for my little cousin. My uncle, a single father going through a divorce, was often busy with work as he was in law enforcement, and I would assist in caring for my cousin, helping her read books, clean the house, and so forth. However, even during those times away, it felt like history was repeating itself for me. Staying for summers with my grandmother and residing downstairs at my uncle's house, where they all lived in a duplex, mirrored the environment I sought to escape. It was a challenging period marked by secrets and lies, compounded by the weight of responsibilities I shouldn't have had at such a young age.

Even during my stay in New York, it felt like I didn't belong there either. I didn't feel like a grandchild; there was a lot of favoritism, and I just didn't feel loved. My grandmother would do my hair and other things, but despite these moments, I felt a disconnect. I remember going to my sister's godmother's house. She would come and get me, and I would stay with them for a few days, but then I didn't want to return to my grandparents' house. My grandparents once put me in a camp across the street from their house, but I didn't feel any love there either. Growing up, I felt like an outsider on that side of the family; there was never any closeness. Despite this, I have memories of playing outside and my grandmother straightening my hair. Although they took me in for the summers, I felt love from my grandfather but not as much from my grandmother. It was just a different time.

Looking back, I vividly remember the constant favoritism towards one grandchild, perhaps because she lived there. I never felt the love, bond, and sense of family that should have been there. It was as if I wasn't treated as a true family member; there was always a sense of separation.

These memories remain vivid in my mind, replaying like scenes from the past. Back then, growing up felt different, and people could be mean. Despite the hardships, those times taught me valuable lessons about life and human nature. There were times when we would travel back and

Pieces of Me

forth to New York, and I always felt like I didn't fit in. Everyone knew Lorraine and Moochie, my sister and brother, because they were in New York a lot, and I was often away. Despite this, I stayed with my grandparents, but my cousins would constantly pick fights with me. There was no real reason for this, but it happened. Being young and having the cousins I had, I faced many challenges. When my mother moved us out of the city to a suburb in another state, it caused some friction within the family. They didn't know how to treat us. My mother, who loved her family deeply, made sure we attended all the family reunions to stay connected. However, my cousins were very mean; they would call me names and never include me in anything. It's crazy to think about how things were back then. It wasn't a pleasant situation at all.

When I was at home with my mother, I would only visit New York with her. But the summer months, when I was away from my mom, were heartbreaking for me. It was during those summers in Brooklyn and Queens that I felt the most pain. While some of my cousins were loving, there were always conflicts after church, leading to fights. I dreaded Sunday mornings because of the strained family dynamics. I often felt like an outcast among my cousins, who seemed to pick on me for no reason. They wouldn't let me join them or would tease me, calling me names and sometimes even trying to hit me. I never understood why. I desperately wanted to fit in, but it was challenging. Perhaps they saw me as different after my mother moved away, but whatever the reason, my interactions with them were never pleasant. All I wanted was to be loved by them and to fit in, but I felt like an outcast compared to my siblings, Lorraine and Moochie. Especially my brother Moochie, who had a different experience. Lorraine was always doing her own thing.

From 1982 to 1984, as I entered my teenage years, the weight of responsibility fell upon me. At just 14, I began working at Burger King, where my mother faithfully dropped me off after school, or I would walk there myself. Despite my tender age, I obtained a worker's permit to serve as a host at Burger King on Drum Hill, earning my keep. By the time I turned 16, I had secured a job at Papa Gino's, a pizza place, where my hourly wage increased from $3.50 to $5.15 an hour. These jobs, though demanding, provided me with a sense of independence. They taught me the value of hard work and perseverance, even despite the challenges of adolescence. When my father lost his job, I felt a greater sense of duty to help support my family. Even after we settled into our new home in Chelmsford, my mother supported me as I juggled work commitments.

Navigating the ups and downs of our family dynamics, I remained steadfast as a pillar of support. While my parents worked towards their spiritual and personal growth, I was responsible for ensuring stability for my younger sibling, Reign, and my niece, Sophia. It was a challenging task I undertook with determination and love.

As life unfolded, my sister Lorraine faced further challenges, ultimately giving birth to another child, Jamel, in the midst of trying to navigate her young marriage. Then, a sudden and confusing event unfolded that would deeply impact Lorraine and all of us. As mentioned earlier, her husband, who had become a central part of her life, unexpectedly vanished. He left under the most mundane of pretenses—claiming he was stepping out to buy a pack of cigarettes—only to never return. His disappearance left a void filled with uncertainty and countless unanswered questions, casting a shadow of perplexity over our family.

This abrupt abandonment forced Lorraine into a situation many feared, but few are ever truly prepared to handle. Alone, without her partner's support, she faced the daunting task of raising her child by herself. The resilience she had always shown took on a new form as she adapted to her new reality. Despite the instability and challenges, she persevered, ensuring her child felt none of the chaos that churned around them.

Our family, too, had to adjust to this new normal. We rallied around Lorraine, offering her the emotional and practical support she needed. This time it tested our strength as a unit, but it also reinforced our commitment to one another. Through it all, Lorraine's courage and our collective resilience shone as beacons of hope in the face of the trials we preserved.

Looking back, I am grateful for the resilience that carried us through the darkest moments and the faith that guided us toward brighter days. Our journey was far from easy, but it was one defined by love, perseverance, and the enduring belief that no challenge is unconquerable with faith and determination.

Even during that time, my sister Lorraine was never back to her norm. Mentally, she struggled with a lot of different things. My nephew Jamel stayed in New York for a while until my mother received a phone call, prompting her to travel to New York to bring him back. With Jamel's arrival, more responsibilities fell on me as we settled into our new life in Chelmsford, Massachusetts.

As I grew up on El Dorado Road, I found myself working at Papa Gino's, a place where my mother often picked me up or dropped me off. When my mother walked in the door, people always noticed her style. She had a knack for style, always sporting a trendy haircut, sometimes even a rat tail during the summer months. It was during this time that I met Gloria, from San Diego, California. Our paths crossed in 1984 when I was just 16 years old, and she was 18 years old. We became special friends.

I remember excitedly telling my mother about Gloria, who was dating a music producer who had a studio in Westford, Massachusetts. Gloria and I would spend time together, often discussing her California roots and her adventures in the music industry. Our friendship blossomed, and I eagerly awaited her visits to the pizza place.

One evening, I was walking to a friend's house after my shift, waiting for my mother to pick me up. It was a convenient meeting point, and my mother would come to collect me from there. On the way, a gentleman named Bruce approached me, asking, "Are you following me?" My sarcastic nature kicked in, and I quickly retorted, "I ain't following you." Despite our exchange, we struck up a conversation. We ended up walking to the same complex and we discovered he was my friend's neighbor.

Bruce moved to the area because he worked for a company called Wang Laboratories. Our initial interaction was marked by my usual sarcastic attitude. Bruce started showing up at the pizza place more frequently, and our conversations turned into a regular occurrence.

Even though Bruce and I merely crossed paths initially—particularly when he used to stop by Papa Gino's for a bite—we gradually saw more of each other. Recognizing his loneliness in the area, being from New York as we were, I invited him to my parents' home. I eventually introduced Bruce to my entire family, offering him a warm welcome to our circle. My mother, always the gracious host, would prepare Sunday dinners and we made sure to call him over. He had no close connections locally, so our invitations were a gesture of warmth, drawing him into the comforting embrace of family. He greatly appreciated my mother's cooking, which only deepened the bond. During these gatherings, Bruce often took on a mentor-like role, constantly reminding me to stay in school and avoid the pitfalls of teenage pregnancy. His advice was always delivered with care, reflecting his wish for me to succeed. Over time, Bruce became a familiar face to my family, almost like an extension of our own. However, as life often goes, our meetings became less frequent, and gradually, Bruce faded from the regular scene of our lives, leaving behind memories of shared meals and meaningful conversations.

Regina Hall

Let me take you back to the days of growing up, where Gloria and I navigated the twists and turns of life with a sense of adventure. From our early encounters to the wild escapades in the studio, our journey was marked by laughter, mischief, and an unbreakable bond. Gloria and I, always the daredevils, found ourselves in the most unexpected situations, often with characters much older than us. Together, we embarked on a whirlwind of experiences, each one more outrageous than the last.

One vivid memory that never fails to bring a smile to my face is our time at the studio. It was always buzzing with activity, filled with musicians and artists of every kind. Gloria, with her undeniable talent, would spend hours pouring her soul into her music, while I soaked in the creative energy around us.

But it wasn't just the music that kept us entertained. Oh no, it was the antics of the people we encountered, like the infamous cousin of Mikkel, Gloria's boyfriend and producer. This character had a penchant for quirky phrases, his favorite being "Ooo-E-Didly Bop." One fateful day, in the middle of the chaos of the studio, he found himself unwittingly caught in a hilarious prank orchestrated by none other than Gloria and me.

As we giggled like mischievous schoolchildren, Mikkel's cousin, Warren's dramatic undressing was interrupted by the sudden and oh so unexpected return of Mikkel, who had stated he would be away for the evening. With lightning speed, we made our escape, leaving behind a bewildered

Pieces of Me

Warren in a state of undress that would surely be the talk of the studio for weeks to come.

Gloria and Mikkel broke up and reconciled often. During my school years, there were times I would play hooky to look out for Gloria, who during one of their breakups stayed and lived with us. She often found herself speaking with a musician from the group Morris Day and the Time, someone we communicated with frequently at that time. During these moments, she would try to sneak away, and I would cover for her. These adventures, woven into our daily lives, culminated in an infamous incident involving potato salad.

One particularly vivid memory stands out: Gloria had decided to make a special dinner for Mikkel's birthday. She spent the afternoon preparing everything, determined to impress him with her cooking. However, things didn't go as planned. In her rush, she accidentally used the wrong mustard in the potato salad. When Mikkel tasted it, his reaction was less than enthusiastic. He looked at Gloria with a puzzled expression and asked, "What is this?"

The absurdity of the mustard mishap was just one part of the larger issues between Gloria and Mikkel, who was significantly older than she was. Fueled by a misstep in mustard choice and a determination to assert her independence, she packed her bags and left Mikkel, armed with nothing but a suitcase and a heart full of courage. She packed her bags, leaving Mikkel alone with nothing but a suitcase and a heart full of regret. Ironically, she took the suitcase she had bought him for his birthday. Despite the separation, Mikkel persistently pursued Gloria, determined to win her back. His persistence won over, and after persuading her to return, he proposed. The two flew to San Diego, California and married in a whirlwind of romance, marking the start of a new chapter for them. Ironically, it was during their honeymoon that Gloria became pregnant.

Looking back, those times were more than just escapades; they were the foundation of our sisterhood, built on trust and the simple joy of looking out for one another. The infamous potato salad incident became a symbol of our mischievous adventures, a reminder of the lengths we would go to protect each other, and the bonds that held us together.

The parallels between our lives were striking, as we both navigated complex relationships and transitions into motherhood around the same time. While Gloria lived with us, we shared many intimate moments—ranging from daily routines to significant life events. My mother often let me spend weekends at the studio, where Gloria and I would sometimes stay the night, especially during her recording sessions. Our bond was incredibly strong; we were not just friends but family.

Our pregnancies only brought us closer. Gloria went into labor first, and I followed just six days later, our children born less than a week apart. I remember traveling to her baby shower in Boston, a 45-minute drive from our home, even though they had a studio in Westford, Massachusetts. These shared experiences underscored the profound connection between us, marking our journeys not just as friends, but as sisters navigating the unpredictable waters of life together. Even though there were challenging times when Gloria stayed with us, they were also full of fun and friendship. My mother played a pivotal role during this period; she was incredibly supportive, providing a safe space where we could discuss anything and everything. There were delightful days filled with impromptu photo shoots, with my mother acting as the photographer, and shopping trips where we picked out playful pajamas. She would organize makeup sessions, ensuring we always looked our best, creating a light-hearted atmosphere that helped balance the complexities of our personal lives. While I held back on revealing the full depth of my own relationship struggles, my mother was more acquainted with Gloria's situation and the complexities of her being with an older man. Her understanding and openness made her easy to confide in, making our home a nurturing environment for honest conversations.

Moreover, as I navigated typical sibling issues with my younger sister—who often ventured into my room and closet without permission—my mother recognized my need for privacy. She allowed me to install a lock on my door and even set up my own phone line, affirming her respect for my growing independence. These privileges were not just about creating physical boundaries; they symbolized my transition beyond my years, as I managed personal spaces and relationships with a maturity that belied my age.

Through it all, one constant remained: the support and understanding of my dear mother. She was more than just a confidante; she was a pillar of strength, a beacon of love and acceptance in a world that often felt chaotic and uncertain. And so, as I reflect on those carefree days of youth, filled with laughter, love, and the occasional misadventure, I am reminded of the precious bonds that tied us together, weaving a tapestry of memories that will forever hold a special place in my heart.

As I grew older, my mother also attempted to provide respite by taking me on trips. One memorable summer, we visited California, staying with family and friends at the Harringtons. Despite the scenic backdrop and fleeting moments of joy, that summer was marred by a traumatic incident. I was in a harrowing situation on a seemingly ordinary outing for a McDonald's apple pie. My aunt's husband, whom I trusted, betrayed that trust in a manner that shook me to my core.

I felt a profound sense of isolation and fear upon returning to the house. I sought refuge in the shower, desperately trying to process what had happened. His words of manipulation only served to deepen the wounds, leaving me yearning for the safety and comfort of my mother's embrace.

The aftermath of that experience continues to haunt me, a stark reminder of the darkness that lurks beneath the surface of seemingly ordinary moments. Yet, during pain and uncertainty, I found resilience. I summoned the courage to speak up, seeking comfort in the familiarity of my cousin's home. I had the opportunity to pursue my dreams and ambitions. Yet, even as I embraced this newfound independence, my memories of our struggles in Chelmsford remained etched.

Pieces of Me

But within the joys of newfound freedom and the promise of a brighter future, the scars of my past lingered. The specter of addiction continued to loom large, a constant reminder of the fragility of our happiness. Yet, through it all, one thing remained constant: the bond that held us together, unbreakable in the face of adversity.

As I reflect on this journey, I am filled with gratitude for the lessons learned and the strength gained along the way. My story is one of resilience and redemption, a testament to the power of love and the indomitable spirit of the human heart.

In sharing my story, I inspire others facing their struggles to remind them that they are not alone and that there is always hope, even in the darkest times. Through our trials, we find our true strength, and through our shared experiences, we find our common humanity.

And so, our journey continues, filled with hope, courage, and the belief that no matter what challenges may lie ahead, as long as we have each other, we can overcome anything.

Affirmation: "I embrace the power of resilience and redemption, knowing that each challenge brings me closer to my true strength and purpose."

Bible Scripture: "The righteous person may have many troubles, but the LORD delivers him from them all." – Psalm 34:19 (NIV)

> "I EMBRACE CHANGE AND WELCOME NEW BEGINNINGS."

_____

_____

_____

_____

_____

_____

_____

_____

_____

_____

Pieces of Me

PIECES OF ME

Chapter 14: Through the Storm: Embracing Motherhood and Finding Strength

As I embark on the following chapters of my book, the focus shifts to a new phase of my life, one filled with unexpected challenges and profound moments of growth. Before delving into the depths of my journey, it's crucial to understand the backdrop against which it all unfolded. As a teenager, I found myself navigating a complex web of responsibilities and relationships. While working at the pizza place and babysitting after school to make ends meet, I became entangled in a relationship with an older man, whose connection to my father added an unexpected layer of complexity.

Looking back, I recall vividly the moments when Gloria and I would spend time at my house, indulging in our mischievous adventures. Sneaking out of the window was our routine, with Gloria's undercover boyfriend adding an extra layer of thrill to our escapades. We embraced the audacity of our youth, engaging in countless antics as we navigated our teenage years. In the mornings, we played our parts, acting as though I had just awoken and climbed back through the window, seamlessly blending into the facade of normalcy. I would return home, ready for school, all the while maintaining the charade of being in a relationship with the older man, even as I was picked up and then returned home. Those moments, lived in the shadow of secrecy, defined my experience of that relationship during my youth.

It was a regular day when he picked me up from school, and we went for a ride in his burgundy Monte Carlo-type car. As we were driving down Chelmsford Street, we encountered a boy riding his bike and crossing the street. Suddenly, the unthinkable happened—the boy was struck by the car. It was a devastating moment as the ambulance rushed to the scene, and the boy was found to have a broken leg. This incident revealed unsettling truths about the man I was with, as I discovered that the car wasn't his roommate's, as he had claimed, but belonged to someone else entirely, as revealed by the woman's name on the registration in the glove compartment. Despite the shock and trauma of the accident, our relationship continued as before, with long phone conversations and attending events together, such as fashion shows and church gatherings.

Despite the challenges I faced, including a turbulent car accident, life took an unexpected turn when I discovered I was pregnant. I met Dreena when I was in middle school. She had just moved from Florida, quickly becoming a familiar face at the school I attended in Chelmsford. Our paths crossed in the bustling hallways, and before long, we struck up a friendship. Despite coming from different backgrounds, there was an instant connection between us, and our bond only grew stronger with each passing day. Alongside our middle school adventures, there were also times when Dreena, my niece Sophia, and I would team up for talent shows, as Dreena had a passion for performing. We would showcase our talents together, bringing a mix of excitement and laughter to each performance. These shared experiences added another layer to our friendship, creating cherished memories that we would look back on fondly.

It was during those nights when I would take out the Pinto given to me by my parents, just to see if I spotted his vehicle. Dreena, my trusty companion, often accompanied me on these nighttime excursions, our eyes scanning the streets for any sign of his familiar car. It became a ritual of sorts, a way for us to gather clues about his whereabouts and activities. And under the darkness of the night, illuminated only by the dim glow of streetlights, we forged a bond of friendship as we navigated the twists and turns of the truth. In the course of the challenging nights of his graveyard shifts and the unsettling discoveries about his other relationships, a new reality began to dawn on me. I confided in my friend Dreena, pouring out the complexities of my situation. Together, we navigated the murky waters of uncertainty, grappling with the weight of my unexpected pregnancy.

As revelations about the true nature of his connections surfaced, I realized the depth of deception woven into our relationship. Armed with a speakerphone and a determination to uncover the truth, I began to tape our conversations, capturing the deceitful web of lies that entangled us. The decision to share these recordings with the other woman and her family was not made lightly, but it was a necessary step in unraveling the facade of dishonesty. Confrontations ensued, culminating in a tense meeting in the parking lot of Zayre's, where I stood my ground, unmasking the deception that had clouded our relationship. Despite the uncertainty of how to confide in my own mother, two steadfast allies stood by my side: Dreena and Gloria. Gloria, with her solid support and resourcefulness, became the bridge between my challenging reality and the comforting embrace of my mother's understanding.

At the age of 18, I found myself thrust into adulthood, navigating the challenges of parenthood. The circumstances of my pregnancy, conceived with an older man, added layers of complexity to an already chaotic time. My parents, both pastors and marriage counselors, provided crucial support during this period of change. However, when the older man entered my life, our interactions took a turn, resulting in a pregnancy that would forever alter my path. As truths emerged, Gloria and I discovered a deeper connection—we were both pregnant, embarking on this journey of motherhood together. United by shared experiences and strong support for each other, our bond grew stronger.

However, alongside all of this, the unexpected news of my pregnancy brought a new dimension to our already complicated relationship. And it was during my senior year that all of these events transpired, adding to the stormy nature of that time in my life. Uncertain of the future and struggling with difficult decisions, I confided in my friend Gloria, setting the stage for the transformative journey that lay ahead.

As a senior in high school, balancing the demands of academics, childcare, and my struggles became increasingly challenging. Despite the weight of my responsibilities, I persevered, taking on roles as a babysitter and daycare staff to make ends meet. Facing the uncertain journey of motherhood was filled with obstacles, yet it also led to moments of profound growth and discovery

It was actually during the time when my mother found out. She had just thrown a big anniversary party, and I was always the one taking care of the other kids since everyone's anniversaries were in the same month as my parents. That evening, after taking all the kids out for ice cream and pizza, I was finally able to hang out with my friends. When I returned home, I noticed the TV on in my bedroom. Since my mother always let me use her car, a Camaro, I never forgot that I had on a white miniskirt when I went out with my friends. As I walked into my room, I found my mother laying on my bed. She got up and closed the door, acting like she was inspecting my stomach or noticing something. In reality, my dearest sister and friend, Gloria, had spilled the beans. Despite the fact that my mother hadn't actually noticed anything, her words were, "I noticed that your stomach," a statement that took me by surprise. It was clear that Gloria's revelation had prompted this conversation. My mother played the role perfectly, skilled at keeping confidences, pretending she hadn't been told anything, even though Gloria had spilled the secret.

Despite our challenges, my friendship with Gloria flourished, strengthened by shared experiences and mutual trust. As Gloria confided in my mother, she unwittingly became a guiding presence in the darkness, illuminating the path forward with her constant support and compassion.

I was definitely caught off guard when my mother broached the topic, informing me that she suspected I might be pregnant and that we were going to get a pregnancy test in the morning from my primary doctor. It was still summertime, and I recall vividly that I was working at a daycare center with little children, my summer job. Before heading to work, I had to drop off a urine specimen in a photo film cup. However, before we even reached the workplace, it was a challenging journey ahead. My mother, supportive yet apprehensive, accompanied me to get the results. When the reality hit, my mother's concern shifted to action as she comforted me while navigating the uncertain path ahead.

The emotional rollercoaster of taking the pregnancy test and waiting for the results was overwhelming. My mother's reassurance offered a glimmer of hope in the midst of the uncertainty, even when she asked, "What are you going to do now that reality has set in?" Though it shifted the weight of the situation onto me, together we braced ourselves for the challenges ahead, knowing we would face them with strength and determination.

After I finished my work shift, my mother picked me up, but instead of heading straight home, she stopped at the store. Between the aisles of Pampers and groceries, the weight of my situation felt heavy. Tears streamed down my face, mirroring the overwhelming emotions swirling within. That evening, after a somber dinner, my mother announced that we were going to confront him. As we stood at his doorstep, my mother unleashed her fury, confronting him about his role in my pregnancy. The truth was laid bare as the woman whose name graced the car registration stood by his side, confirming the depth of his deception. My mother's words rang out in the night air, a testament to her fierce protection and dedicated love. Within the chaos, I found myself caught between their heated exchange, the tension suffocating. Outside, overwhelmed by the intensity of the moment, I collapsed, the weight of it all crashing down on me.

Before my mother and I could reach home to break the news, the older man had already called my father to tell him I was pregnant. As we walked in, the atmosphere was heavy, the dust of revelation barely settled. My father's voice pierced the silence—we could hear his words a blend of anger and disappointment that echoed down the phone line at the older man. It was a harsh reminder of the consequences that come with deceit and betrayal. In that charged moment, I grappled with the magnitude of the situation, unsure of the path ahead. My father had placed his trust in the older man, who often played the keyboards at our church after my father found a building for our congregation. This trust was now shattered, revealing the painful complexity of our intertwined lives.

During my pregnancy, I was determined to continue my education, supported by a tutor—an older lady who came daily to bring my assignments and help me study. This dedicated assistance allowed me to graduate from high school on time, despite the challenges of expecting my daughter. Although I had earned a scholarship to UCLA, thanks to my achievements in track during high school, I had to make the difficult decision to decline it. Instead, I enrolled at UMass, a choice influenced by my circumstances but still aligned with my educational goals. My parents reassured me that despite this detour, I could still pursue my academic ambitions. However, this change wasn't without its emotional costs, and there were moments of profound disappointment.

At home, conversations with my mom about the future were bittersweet. I would often ask her, "What do you think I'm having?" and she confidently predicted a girl, to whom I planned to give the name Sarita. My mother's support was never failing, yet there were times when the weight of the situation brought her frustration to the surface. I'll never forget one quiet afternoon at home, six months into my pregnancy, when the stress momentarily overwhelmed her. She expressed her disappointment loudly, revealing her deep concerns about the unexpected path my life had taken. While I understood her feelings—rooted in the hopes she had harbored for me—it was a clear reminder of the complex emotions, my situation evoked.

During that period of uncertainty, I frequently turned to my brother, Moochie, also known as Theodore Mitchell, for support and guidance. He was a steadfast presence in my life, always ready to lend an ear and offer sage advice. I vividly recall his visit to town, during which I confided in him about my pregnancy and the challenges I was facing. His persistent support provided comfort in the midst of chaos, reassuring me that I was not alone in navigating the complexities of motherhood.

Pieces of Me

In the face of uncertainty, my journey as a young mother began, filled with obstacles to overcome and moments of profound growth and discovery. As I navigated the complexities of motherhood, I was reminded of the power of resilience and the strength that lies within. And so, as the next chapter of my story unfolds, it is a testament to the enduring power of love and the unbreakable bond between mother and child.

When my brother returned to Massachusetts it marked a significant chapter in my pregnancy journey, supported every step of the way by my devoted family. My mother, the epitome of nurturing care, organized a heartfelt baby shower to commemorate the impending arrival of my daughter. During this time, my brother, who had started dating Artemis—a woman he had met in Roxbury, Boston—made sporadic appearances at my Lamaze classes, though he often left early, seeking comfort from his frustrations with Artemis.

On December 28, 1986, just days after Christmas, my brother made a decision that would change the course of events. Rather than attending Lamaze classes with me, he chose to visit his girlfriend. As my mother dropped him off at the train station in Lowell to head to Boston, little did we know that our plans would soon be disrupted. On our journey back home, my water broke, signaling the onset of labor. Despite the challenges of pregnancy, I remained steadfast in my job at the clothing store, managing my responsibilities with never-failing determination. Thanks to a tutor arranged by my mother and the school, I was able to maintain my studies and graduate high school, despite the physical limitations imposed by my growing stomach. My baby shower, attended by friends and church family, was a joyous occasion filled with love and anticipation. However, as my due date approached, I found myself unexpectedly going into labor earlier than expected, on December 28th instead of January 1st. Despite the surprise, my family rallied around me, offering support and a source of comfort during the chaos. In the throes of childbirth, moments of cheerfulness emerged, including a comical interaction with my mother, who couldn't resist pulling my hair in her excitement. Despite the challenges, the delivery room was filled with laughter and love as I welcomed my daughter, Sarita, into the world.

In that moment of panic and uncertainty, the absence of my brother weighed heavily on my mind. With the realization sinking in that he wouldn't be present for the birth of my daughter, Sarita, anxiety gripped me. However, as I found myself in the delivery room, surrounded by my mother and the supportive presence of Ann, a supervisor from another store where I had worked, I drew strength from their enduring support.

Ann had always been more than just a supervisor; she had offered me a management position at Pants Place Plus, at the shoe department, recognizing my dedication and work ethic from my time at the clothing Store called 5-7-9. Despite the challenges of my pregnancy, she stood by me, providing regular support and care. As labor pains intensified, Ann's reassuring presence provided a sense of comfort during childbirth. And as I reflect on that unforgettable day, I am reminded of the invaluable role my family and friends played in guiding me through one of life's most profound experiences. Yet, the joy of impending motherhood, a harsh truth emerged. The father of my unborn child had deceived me. While I sat alone in my bedroom, six months pregnant, I received the devastating news that he had married another woman. The betrayal cut deep, leaving me grappling with heartbreak and betrayal.

Confronting him alongside my mother was a moment of reckoning. His deception and duplicity laid bare, revealing the extent of his betrayal. As I navigated the aftermath of his deceit, I found comfort in the dedicated love of my community, who rallied around me during my baby shower and the christening of my daughter, Sarita Aishaa'.

Throughout the challenging months of my pregnancy, my brother, residing in New York as a social worker, became my confidant, offering a listening ear and words of encouragement during my darkest moments. Around the six-month mark of my pregnancy, a call to the church on a Saturday afternoon revealed a wedding ceremony taking place—an event that would later have significant implications for my life.

Following Sarita's birth, tensions escalated as the older man and his new wife expressed a desire to visit. Sensing the need to protect me, my brother confronted the situation head-on, firmly defending our family's integrity and refusing to let them dismiss Sarita's paternity. Despite initial challenges, the older man later acknowledged Sarita as his own, expressing remorse for the turmoil he had caused. These incidents serve as pivotal moments that shape the dynamics of my journey, highlighting the resilience and strength of my family in the face of adversity.

As I navigated the challenges of impending motherhood, life took unexpected twists and turns, shaping the course of my journey in profound ways. Despite the hurdles I faced, the strong support of my family served as a guiding light in the uncertainty.

In the excitement of my high school graduation and the anticipation of a promising future, the news of my pregnancy cast a shadow over my plans. Though I had been accepted to college, the realities of impending motherhood forced me to put my dreams on hold. As I prepared to welcome my daughter into the world, the support of my parents, especially my father Benjamin, became invaluable.

As time passed, Bruce re-entered my life unexpectedly. One day, I stopped by his apartment complex, and we chatted by his window. During our conversation, I never mentioned that I had a child; it was a detail I hesitated to share just yet. After our talk, Bruce decided to visit, likely curious and wanting to reconnect further. Coincidentally, I wasn't home when he arrived; I had stepped out for a moment. It was my sister, Reign, who enthusiastically took the opportunity to introduce him to Sarita. "Oh, do you want to see Regina's new baby?" she asked him. Bruce, taken aback, responded in surprise, "A baby? What baby?" And when Reign said, "Regina's," his astonishment deepened. "What?" he exclaimed, clearly shocked by the news. In that spontaneous moment, Reign bridged the gap I had left, inadvertently making Bruce one of the first persons outside our immediate family to meet my daughter.

Despite the challenges I faced, I found strength in my daughter's love and my spirit's resilience. Graduating from high school as a young mother was a testament to my determination to overcome adversity and pursue a brighter future for myself and my child.

Yet, as I celebrated my achievements, my parents' marriage began to unravel, casting a shadow over our family's stability. Dysfunction crept into our household, leading to tensions and a separation. However, this time also marked the beginning of significant upheaval for my family. As my parents neared divorce, my father's sister, who lived with us, caused tension with her deceit and betrayal, despite my mother's generous efforts to provide for her, even buying her clothes. The betrayal deeply wounded my mother, whose health declined as she lost weight from stress and depression. Determined to start over, she saw leaving the family home as the only way forward, though it meant leaving me behind.

Despite the upheaval, I remained steadfast in my resolve to create a better life for myself and my daughter, drawing strength from the love and support of those around me.

In the face of betrayal, heartbreak, and upheaval, I emerged stronger, and more determined than ever to forge my path and create a future filled with hope and promise. With Sarita by my side, I embarked on the next chapter of my journey, ready to face whatever challenges lay ahead with courage and resilience. Even after my daughter was born, her presence brought unexpected benefits, like fully funded home improvements that my parents were eligible for due to new family assistance programs. Throughout this period, I balanced motherhood with education, supported by a tutor, who charged only a modest fee, and visited me daily to assist with my assignments while I cared for my daughter.

Legal challenges with Sarita's father led us to engage a lawyer and initiate court proceedings in 1986. The judge ordered the older man to pay $125 weekly for child support, which helped me secure childcare for my daughter so I could attend classes at the University of Massachusetts and continue my education.

Affirmation: "I learn from my rushed decisions, gaining wisdom and strength for the future."

Bible Scripture: "The Lord makes firm the steps of the one who delights in him; though he may stumble, he will not fall, for the Lord upholds him with his hand." - Psalm 37:23-24 (NIV)

Pieces of Me

> "I FIND JOY AND BEAUTY IN THE PRESENT MOMENT."

Regina Hall

_____

_____

_____

_____

_____

_____

_____

_____

_____

_____

_____

_____

PIECES OF ME

Chapter 15: Rushed Decisions, Hard Lessons

I was deeply involved in helping with my father's limousine service and managing household responsibilities. My mother, consistently involved with the church, often sought guidance from her pastor during these trying times, leaning on her faith as a cornerstone of her strength.

The first birthday party for my daughter, a moment of joy, was held at our home. My parents were going through difficult times and eventually lost their home. As they were reconciling, they moved out and decided not to take me along, leaving me in an empty house with only the bedroom set I had purchased. I vividly remember having some milk, but no refrigerator, and I survived on peanut butter and jelly sandwiches.

"During my pregnancy, I had a wonderful tutor who took a special interest in me. She, along with her husband, made sure I was okay, often visiting me in the empty house and providing much-needed support and care.

Bruce, re-entering my life, would stop by, and, despite his emotional state, I always assured him that I would be okay. Many times, I didn't understand why things happened the way they did or why I was left behind, but these experiences shaped who I am today despite the difficulties. As I recount my journey and the turbulence of my past, I realize that I discovered gratitude which gave way to moments of stability and newfound purpose. During the uncertainty of my homelessness, a strength within me emerged, guiding me toward a semblance of stability and security.

Amid these hardships, I moved into a homeless shelter to rebuild our lives. Bruce became a steadfast source of support. His commitment deepened when he saw the stark conditions I was enduring, and he was moved to tears by the situation.

Bruce made sure I was taken care of, even when I had to put milk in the window during cold days. Though the house was empty and everyone else had moved into a condo, I still had electricity. Eventually, I went to a shelter. I was able to store my belongings in Dreena's mother's attic for $60 a month, or $15 a week. Some items went missing when I moved out of the shelter, but I survived and created many memories.

During my time in the shelter on Pawtucket Blvd. in Lowell, MA, I was determined to finish school. Though I couldn't complete my college degree then, I managed to earn an associate degree. A kind Puerto Rican woman took me under her wing, helping me navigate through those tough times. Bruce would visit often, worried about me, until the day I told him I finally got a place. Patricia continued to support me, picking me up for classes and ensuring my daughter was safely with the babysitter, a dear friend's mother who watched her for $50 a week, which I could afford with the child support automatically garnished from her father's paycheck.

Pieces of Me

Despite my challenges, I pressed on, determined to carve out a better life for myself and my daughter. With my friend Patricia's support, she picked me up and helped me get to school at Lowell University, known today as the University of Massachusetts, she became a true friend. We had known each other growing up because our parents knew each other well. My mother, Dolores, and her mother, Lorraine, were both strict, ensuring they always knew our whereabouts. When I became pregnant and had my daughter, Patricia was there for me, providing a helping hand. While I was living in a shelter, she made sure my daughter and I were taken care of, often dropping us off at a friend's mother's house, who became my daughter's caretaker. As I sought refuge in a shelter, I confronted the harsh realities of my circumstances, grappling with feelings of despair and uncertainty. Yet, amidst the darkness, a glimmer of hope emerged as I embarked on self-discovery and renewal.

With the help of the Puerto Rican woman, I eventually secured a new apartment at 42 Marshall Street, Apt 8, under a housing program similar to Section 8. It was called 707 at the time. With her help, I found refuge in a humble apartment furnished with love and memories from my past. Though many items were hand-me-downs, I made it work until I could improve my situation. This new beginning was a ray of hope in the midst of the storm, allowing me to stabilize my life and provide a stable home for my daughter. Every single day of the week, Patricia ensured I got from point A to point B, picking me up every morning in her car.

By the time I had established myself in my new apartment and was well settled into my new role and apartment, my friend Jessica and I reconnected. We supported each other as single mothers navigating similar challenges. During this time, I began working as an administrative assistant at WANG Laboratories, a job that a friend, Linda, helped me secure by vouching for me. Before this position, I worked at a childcare center, but the job at WANG allowed me to earn more money and better support my daughter.

Through all these trials, my relationship with Bruce grew stronger, offering a reassuring constant amid the flux. Together, we faced the challenges of rebuilding a life marked by resilience and the support of those who believed in us.

As my relationship with Bruce grew, he increasingly assumed a paternal role, often overstepping by advising Jessica and me on personal matters such as shopping, which we resisted. During this time, Jessica moved in with me after being dropped off by a friend. She brought some of her belongings over in a car, a practical arrangement especially after I lost my job at Wang Laboratories. I had not reported my income while receiving food stamps, unaware that it was required, and this oversight costed me the position.

Despite these setbacks, my mother remained a steadfast support, especially when it came to Sarita. One of her friends, whom I used to babysit for, offered to sell me a couch and coffee table for $100. This support was crucial as I navigated the ups and downs with Bruce, including breakups and reconciliations. On one occasion, finding Bruce absent from his apartment, I climbed through an open window to leave him a note and flowers in an attempt to mend our relationship. I later told my brother about this, and shortly afterward, Bruce's stereo equipment, newly purchased from New York, went missing. Given the timing and circumstances, we had to consider the possibility that my brother was involved in the theft.

Amid these personal dramas, I continued to travel to New York with Bruce, accompanied by my daughter Sarita, who was becoming an integral part of his life. During one trip, Bruce's grandmother advised me to leave him due to our ongoing issues. She felt that her grandson was not good for me. We would have great conversations, and I confided in her about my struggles. She listened and offered advice, often encouraging me to reconsider my relationship with Bruce. She said, "You shouldn't stay with him," and her words began to resonate with me.

Bruce and his grandmother often disagreed, but she and I found common ground in our concerns. The time away from Bruce allowed me to reflect on my life. At 20 years old, I was beginning to see things differently. My social life included outings to the NCO club at Fort Devens and nights out with friends from hair school, providing a necessary escape from my responsibilities. Bruce, being older, always tried to act like he was somebody's father. Though we had a relationship, the dynamic was becoming strained. Sometimes, I would stay at his house, and other times he would stay at mine, but it was becoming clear that this arrangement was not sustainable.

Bruce was always there when Sarita's father missed his child support payments, a recurring issue that drove me up the wall. Sarita was often neglected by her father, especially after he decided to remarry and allowed his new wife to call the shots. Due to his other children—not by me, as I only had one child by him—she always made it all about her children, sidelining the ones he had outside of their marriage. He had other children before he married her, but she ensured he was not involved with them. This neglect was not just frustrating—it was heartbreaking. The older man would often ask Bruce, "When are you going to marry her?" Bruce would shoot him a look that said he had lost his mind because he knew that if Sarita's father didn't step up and fulfill his responsibilities, I would go ballistic on Sarita's father.

There was a moment of pure frustration that still lingers in my memory. One day, I decided to take the training wheels off Sarita's bike, hoping to give her a sense of freedom and confidence. However, my anger got the better of me, and in a fit of rage, I grabbed one of the training wheels and deliberately shattered the windshield of the older man's car. This wasn't just about the bike or the car; it was about Sarita's father, who continuously missed his payments and expected me to cover for him with flimsy excuses like taking sick time. The weight of his irresponsibility bore down on me, and despite his failures, Sarita was still his responsibility. The incident with the car was a culmination of my pent-up frustration with his constant letdowns and the overwhelming burden it placed on my shoulders.

Pieces of Me

I ensured my daughter was well taken care of, but he was always trying to pass his responsibilities onto another man. Bruce said, "I have nothing to do with this." Despite everything, I never stopped Sarita's father from seeing her. I would get her ready on weekends for him to pick her up, but he would never show up. Eventually, I gave up on expecting him to be the parent he was supposed to be.

As the tides shifted, Bruce and I found ourselves at a crossroads, our paths diverging as we grappled with the capacity of our relationship. Despite our best efforts, our bond could not withstand the weight of our struggles. We parted ways, each embarking on our own journey of self-discovery and growth. Our circumstances and the nature of our relationship, not as boyfriend and girlfriend but something that was not meant to last, led us to this point of separation.

The combination of these pressures led me to a point where I had to make a difficult decision for the sake of my daughter's well-being and my own peace of mind, that Bruce and my relationship had come to its natural end.

Affirmation: "I learn from my rushed decisions, gaining wisdom and strength for the future."

Bible Scripture: "The LORD makes firm the steps of the one who delights in him, though he may stumble, he will not fall, for the LORD upholds him with his hand." – Psalm 37:23-24 (NIV)

"I AM PROUD OF MY JOURNEY AND THE PERSON I AM BECOMING."

_____

_____

_____

_____

_____

_____

_____

_____

_____

PIECES OF ME

Pieces of Me

PIECES OF ME

Chapter 16: Seeking Refuge and Finding Strength

This phase of my life was marked by rapid changes and intense emotions, from dealing with Bruce and the instability of our relationship to navigating the complexities of new and ending relationships. Each experience, whether challenging or supportive, shaped the next steps I would take, always aiming to provide the best possible life for Sarita and myself.

As I reflect on my journey, I am filled with a profound gratitude for the challenges I have overcome and the lessons I have learned along the way. Through hardship and heartache, I have discovered the depths of my strength and the power of resilience to triumph over adversity.

During this rough period, Dreena introduced me to a man who would eventually become my ex-husband. After reconnecting a year later, our relationship quickly progressed to marriage—a decision made hastily that I later questioned. Concurrently, Sarita's father failed in his responsibilities, leading to confrontations.

And so, as I turned the page on this chapter of my life, I did so with a renewed sense of purpose and determination, ready to face whatever challenges that might lie ahead with courage and conviction. For I knew that no matter what obstacles came my way, I became stronger than I ever imagined, and I continued to rise, time and time again.

Sarita, my beautiful daughter, has been the light of my life, bringing joy, purpose, and hope into my world. Her laughter and smile chased away the shadows of doubt and fear, reminding me of the beauty in every moment. Sarita's presence still fills our home with love, and her strength inspires me daily. She is the embodiment of body, silence, and strength, a constant source of comfort and resilience.

The name Sarita, a diminutive form of the Hebrew name Sarah, means "princess." This name carries a profound significance for me. Just as a princess is a cherished and revered figure, Sarita holds a precious place in my heart, symbolizing the regal joy and purpose she has brought into my life since the moment she was born. Additionally, Sarita can be associated with the Sanskrit word "Saritā," meaning "river," which beautifully aligns with my love for water and the ocean.

Water, to me, is a source of comfort and reflection. I find comfort in sitting by the ocean, gathering my thoughts and finding peace. Naming her Sarita was a tribute to this serene and reflective space in my life. Her name embodies the continuous flow of love and strength she brings into my world, much like a river that sustains life and provides tranquility. Through her, I am reminded of the power of love and the importance of cherishing every moment we have together.

As she grew, so did the love I felt for her, deepening with each passing day. Her curiosity and boundless energy filled our home with warmth and laughter, radiating an indomitable spirit. Despite the rocky and uncertain path, we often traveled, she remained steadfast in her resolve, a ray of hope in the storms. Her unfaltering belief in me became my guiding light, illuminating the darkest corners of my soul and leading me toward a brighter tomorrow.

Looking back, I am filled with profound gratitude for the gift of her presence in my life. She became my inspiration, motivation, and the reason I kept pushing forward, even when the odds were stacked against us. Sarita, my darling daughter, was loved beyond measure and cherished beyond words. Together, we navigated life's ups and downs, and I stood by her side, cheering her on and supporting her every step of the way. With her strength and resilience, there was nothing we could not overcome. We weathered the storms and reveled in the sunshine, knowing that no matter what lay ahead, we would face it together, hand-in-hand, mother and daughter, forever.

Living together, Jessica and I embarked on a journey of mutual support and friendship, always offering a helping hand in times of need. With her by my side, I found comfort in knowing that I was not alone and that together, we could weather any storm that came our way.

Despite the complexities and uncertainties of my past, I found myself drawn to this new possibility, eager to embrace the promise of a fresh start.

Sarita, my beloved daughter, was two years old when I began navigating the delicate balance between my newfound relationship and the remnants of my past. Bruce lingered on the periphery of my life, a constant reminder of the struggles I had endured. Yet, I remained steadfast in my resolve to forge ahead.

Reflecting on this part of my life story, it all began when a childhood friend, Dreena, introduced me to a military man stationed at Fort Devens, MA. Although I met him a year earlier, our connection wasn't significant until our paths crossed again, and he invited me out.

It was in mid-fall when I went out one evening with some friends to the NCO club. After leaving the club, I became acquainted with another gentleman, and we started getting to know each other better.

As we moved forward, the date of December 3rd, 1998, began a significant transformation in my journey. When I introduced my parents to the military man, their approval was swift and firm. With their blessings, we embarked on a whirlwind romance, culminating in a simple yet heartfelt wedding ceremony officiated by my father, Benjamin. Surrounded by loved ones, we exchanged vows, setting the stage for a new chapter.

However, as the dust settled and reality set in, cracks began appearing in our fledgling marriage's facade. With my husband receiving orders to deploy to Germany, our relationship was thrust into the crucible of distance and uncertainty. During the turmoil, I found comfort in my studies at hair school, clinging to a semblance of normalcy in the middle of the chaos.

This period highlighted the rushed nature of my marriage to my ex-husband and the underlying issues due to our lack of familiarity. Despite my reservations, my parents were involved, pushing for the marriage despite knowing I didn't truly know him when I introduced him to my family. Their interference only added to the complexities and challenges of our relationship, which was never meant to be.

During my enrollment in hair school and occasional visits to the club on the military base at Fort Devens, I crossed paths with another man. Despite being married and my husband's impending deployment to Germany, I found myself involved with this new person, influenced by the expectations my parents had set for me. As I grappled with the complexities of my relationships, I faced a devastating miscarriage during my pregnancy. The experience was traumatic; I discovered I was carrying twins and lost one fetus. My sister Lorraine bravely helped retrieve the lost fetus, and together, we brought it to the hospital.

As I prepared to travel overseas while five months pregnant, deemed high risk but permitted to fly, I embarked on a journey to Germany. Upon arrival, I found myself ensnared in an abusive marriage, with my husband's actions leading to frequent hospitalizations due to stress. Reflecting on our rushed marriage, I realized that I barely knew him when we decided to tie the knot. Over time, we both understood that marrying was a mistake. The abuse I endured took a toll on me, and eventually, I gave birth to my daughter Kayla. However, doubts lingered about whether she was truly my husband's child, given the circumstances of her conception. Despite the uncertainty, I knew deep down that the marriage was not healthy for me.

I faced a pivotal decision after my miscarriage when the doctor suggested a Dilation and Curettage (D&C) procedure, which was deemed unnecessary due to the absence of heavy bleeding. Opting against it, I later discovered that I was carrying twins. Choosing not to proceed with the D&C allowed one of the embryos to develop into a healthy child, despite the initial complications and confusion. This decision, supported by my loved ones, marked a significant turning point in my journey.

As I settled into my life in Germany, we did have some good family moments where my ex-husband genuinely wanted to be a supportive husband and father. During this time, we shared a certain bond, doing things together as a family, taking care of our home, and raising our children. We worked as a team, managing household chores and responsibilities. I took on the role of money manager, ensuring everything was in order. Despite these positive aspects, there was an underlying issue that my ex-husband couldn't grasp—how to be a husband without resorting to abuse. This failure to understand this key element of a healthy marriage created a significant strain on our relationship, overshadowing the good moments we had as a family.

Life in Germany presented challenges beyond my expectations. My husband's upbringing and past experiences seemed to manifest in his behavior, particularly his jealousy, which made our life together difficult. Despite the hardships, I remained in Germany, striving to raise my daughters in a foreign land. We resided in Bad Kreuznach, where Kayla was born prematurely due to the strain of the abuse and marital complications, forcing me into early labor.

Surrounded by the chaos, I found myself spending less time in the base quarters with him, seeking refuge elsewhere. Despite my hopes for improvement, the situation only worsened over time. His abusive behavior persisted, compounded by instances of infidelity on his part. His military rank as a sergeant granted him undue influence over others, leading to uncomfortable situations where his behavior became increasingly erratic and unpredictable.

I vividly remember incidents where he acted irrationally, such as confronting individuals who dared to look at me or endangering both of our lives during reckless stunts. These events, coupled with his tendency to resort to violence during social gatherings, created an atmosphere of fear and uncertainty in our home. Despite my efforts to comprehend and reconcile with this side of him, I found myself trapped in a cycle of abuse and despair, grappling with the realization that I barely knew the person I had married.

During the stormy atmosphere of our marriage, I found myself entangled in conflicts with other women who claimed connections to my husband. They would call our home, initially feigning friendship before revealing unsettling truths about their relationships with him. One such encounter led to a confrontation at the NCO club, where I confronted a woman who had been involved with my husband. In a fit of rage and youthful impulsiveness, I engaged in a physical altercation with her.

Returning home, I faced the repercussions of my actions, including threats and attempts at physical violence from my husband. However, this was just another cycle in our rocky relationship. Despite his initial anger, he would always revert to apologies and promises of change, perpetuating the cycle of abuse.

As the years passed, we eventually left Germany behind, but the scars of our troubled marriage remained. I felt unable to seek help from the military authorities, fearing the financial repercussions of reporting the abuse. In the military world, any disciplinary action, such as an Article 15, could result in a reduction in pay or other punitive measures. Thus, I felt compelled to keep our struggles hidden, unable to share the truth about the abuse I endured.

After leaving Germany when Kayla was three and Sarita was five, turning six, we ended up in Kansas. During this time, I returned to the States to take custody of my niece, Sophia, and she became a part of our family. We first settled in Germany and then received orders to go to Fort Riley, Kansas. In Kansas, I focused on trying to make life stable and manageable, attending counseling and striving to improve our marriage. Despite these efforts, the challenges persisted, and I continued to navigate the complexities of our relationship while raising my children and providing a sense of normalcy throughout the ongoing struggles.

After entering Fort Riley, Kansas, the complexities of my marriage continued to unfold. My ex-husband frequently went to the field for military duties. We made our new home, and since he was from St. Louis, Missouri, we often traveled back and forth to visit his family in Kansas City, making weekend trips. Upon returning from Germany, we moved into apartments on Jefferson Avenue in Junction City, Kansas, until we got quarters on the base. During our 30-day leaves to the States, I would visit my parents and other family members.

During these trips and efforts to work on our marriage, I became pregnant again with my daughter, Sierra. As time went on, I also found employment. Initially, during our first tour in Germany, I was a childcare provider, taking care of children full-time in my home. Later, I started working part-time at a childcare center on base, marking the beginning of my career with the government. When we moved to Fort Riley, Kansas, despite the challenges, I was hoping that things would improve. However, the abusive and violent nature of our relationship persisted. My ex-husband continued to struggle with his violent behavior, often putting his hands on me. This led me to call my brother, who came down to Kansas to stay with us, providing support and protection during this difficult time.

As things went on during our four-year tour in Kansas, we had family functions and helped various family members. My brother, who had come to support me, ended up getting a trailer and a job to be close by. We also took care of my ex-husband's nephew who came to visit. Our household was dedicated to supporting and taking care of children, trying to maintain a pleasant family atmosphere despite the difficulties. However, my ex-husband's past experiences and behaviors led to a relationship marred by abuse. Despite his behavior, I stayed, hoping for better days.

We eventually received orders to return to Germany, this time stationed in Baumholder. Shortly after arriving, my ex-husband received orders to deploy to Bosnia. During his deployment, I had to manage the household and care for our three daughters on my own. When he returned, the abuse continued. His jealousy often led to violent outbursts, and our relationship became increasingly untenable.

During this time, I sent my two older daughters to stay with my mother for the summer. However, my sister caused problems that prevented my mother from seeing the children. In October 1997, I returned to the United States for Jessica's wedding and decided to start our separation. Despite his resistance, I knew staying would only lead to more harm. My mother visited and was upset, believing I was breaking up our home. I didn't disclose the full extent of the abuse until after I had left, understanding that leaving was the best decision for my safety and well-being.

The significant changes in my life began in the summer of 1997. My children had left to visit family in Mississippi and then Virginia. I stayed in Germany with Sierra, repeatedly asking my ex-husband about my orders to return to the States. He resisted, making excuses that the sergeant responsible for my orders was on leave. Fortunately, working for a lieutenant allowed me to find out where my orders were, and in October 1997, I finally left for the United States.

Pieces of Me

I went to New York, the Bronx, with my furniture items scheduled for delivery to Fort Dix, New Jersey. My mother, concerned about raising my children in New York, urged me to come to Virginia. I found a townhouse and faxed the necessary lease documents from a pharmacy. After spending Christmas in New York, I moved to Virginia with my children, starting anew.

As things began to unfold, I secured a job with a financial institution while applying to return to government work. On July 27, 1998, my life took a devastating turn. That evening, I wasn't feeling well and asked my boss if I could leave early from training. It was 9:45 pm when I headed home.

When I got home, instead of receiving my usual call from my mother, I received a call from my nephew Jamel, who told me, "Grandma is dead." Initially, I thought he meant my grandmother, but he was talking about my mother. I was in shock and disbelief. My car was in for service, so I had a rental—a Monte Carlo. I ran downstairs and told my brother Moochie, "We gotta go, something is wrong with Mommy." We drove quickly, and a police officer escorted us with his siren on.

Upon arriving at my mother's house, I saw my father standing in the doorway. My brother ran in, trying to find her, but she wasn't there. The police suggested she might have had a heart attack, but we knew better. We rushed to the hospital, where I heard someone calling my name. In the emergency room, I found my mother with tubes, the medical staff trying to revive her. That moment marked the unraveling of my life, as everything changed dramatically from that point onward.

Affirmation: "In seeking refuge, I find strength and courage to rebuild my life."

Bible Scripture: "Whoever dwells in the shelter of the Most High will rest in the shadow of the Almighty. I will say of the LORD, 'He is my refuge and my fortress, my God, in whom I trust.'" - Psalm 91:1-2 (NIV)

Pieces of Me

> I NURTURE MY MIND, BODY, AND
> SOUL WITH LOVE AND COMPASSION

PIECES OF ME

Regina Hall

_____

_____

_____

_____

_____

_____

_____

_____

_____

_____

_____

_____

_____

PIECES OF ME

Conclusion and Next Steps

Stay tuned, stay reflective, and stay excited for the next series of my book. The best is yet to come.

Conclusion of "*Pieces of Me.*"

As you turn the final page of "*Pieces of Me,*" remember that this is merely the first step in a profound journey. This book is part of a series that delves into the heart of our shared human experience, and there is so much more to come.

The next book, "*Naked,*" will strip away the layers even further, revealing raw truths and intimate insights that have shaped my life. We will journey together through vulnerability and strength, uncovering secrets and finding healing in the honesty of our stories.

Reflect on your own journey as you wait for the next installment. Use the journal pages at the end of each chapter to capture your thoughts, emotions, and revelations. What hidden truths do you carry? What chapters of your life are yet to be written? How can embracing your vulnerability lead to profound growth and transformation?

This series is an exploration of resilience, love, and the unyielding human spirit. With each book, we will delve deeper into the complexities of life, emerging stronger and more connected than ever before. "*Pieces of Me*" is just the beginning—prepare yourself for the revelations and growth that await in "*Naked*."

Thank you for sharing in this journey with me. Your story is as important as mine, and together, we will uncover the beauty and strength within every chapter of our lives. The next part of our adventure is on the horizon, and I can't wait to continue this journey with you. Stay tuned, stay reflective, and stay excited for the next series of my book. The best is yet to come.

Follow Echoes in Healing

Website: Watch for the rest of the series and let us know what you think!

www.echoesinhealing.org

Instagram: Post pictures with you holding your book!

https://www.instagram.com/echoesinhealing?igsh=MWV3ZWxobTQ1eGhzZA%3D%3D&utm_source=qr

Facebook: Share your stories and how this series has blessed and impacted you in a positive way!

https://www.facebook.com/profile.php?id=61561417514045&mibextid=LQQJ4d

References for Therapists

Covenant Life Counseling3 LLC
John Hairston, MS, Pre-LAPC
Clinical Therapist, Mental Health counselor specializing in Marriage and Family Therapy.
j.r.hairston4@gmail.com
470.249.4903

Drive -By Therapy
Dr. LaTasha Russell
Social Scientist
Racial Justice Consultant
Doctor of Clinical Psychology
The Association of Black Psychologists
President, South Florida Chapter
Contact: 510-798-2725 Email: lrussellpsyd@gmail.com
Website: www.drivebytherapy.org
Facebook and IG Instagram @doctortasha

About the Author

R – Resilient through every challenge
E – Endurance in the face of adversity
G – Graceful in overcoming obstacles
I – Inspirational to those around her
N – Navigating life with purpose
A – Achieving dreams against all odds

Regina Hall, a native New Yorker from Brooklyn, is a phenomenal woman whose life story exemplifies strength and success. As a devoted mother and grandmother, she has navigated countless challenges, transforming each obstacle into a stepping-stone toward her aspirations. With over three decades of dedicated service to the government, Regina has demonstrated exceptional commitment and endurance.

In 2011, Regina reached a pivotal milestone by earning her degree, symbolizing her relentless pursuit of personal and educational growth. More than twenty years ago, she achieved the dream of homeownership, marking a significant personal victory. As the matriarch of her family, Regina has been a pillar of strength, offering guidance, support, and leadership to her loved ones.

Regina Hall

Regina's journey has led her to become a certified life coach, business coach, financial coach, and business consultant. She uses her expertise to empower and inspire others, offering a guiding hand to those in need. Her impressive career includes managing celebrities, authors, and numerous individuals, highlighting her extraordinary talent in leadership and mentorship. Now, she embarks on a new journey, focusing on her own dreams and aspirations of sharing her story with the world and inspiring others that anything is possible through faith, persistence, and grit.